There Must Be Fifty Ways To Tell Your Mother

Lynn Sutcliffe

For a catalogue or related titles in our
Sexual Politics list please write to us
at the address below:

Cassell plc
Wellington House, 125 Strand
London, WC2R 0BB

PO Box 605
Herndon, VA 20172
USA

First published 1995
Reprinted 1996

British Library Cataloguing-in-Publication Data
A catalogue record for this book is available from the British Library.

ISBN 0-304-33112-0

Typeset by Ronald Clark
Printed and bound in Great Britain by
Biddles Ltd, Guildford and King's Lynn

CONTENTS

ACKNOWLEDGEMENTS

I am indebted to everyone who agreed to be interviewed for this book. I am extremely grateful that you entrusted me with your stories, and I hope you consider that I have done our history justice.

David, thank you so much for your vital encouragement and for being computerless for many more months than anticipated. I am also very grateful to Jon and Amanda for the use of both their printers. Fernando, I would like to acknowledge the invaluable inspiration gained from our early brainstorms. Sonya, a big thank you for letting me use the title from our show and for your support. Michelle, you are the only person I know who always has a score of *The Wizard of Oz* to hand. Mac, you were a wonderful cover-boy.

Sarah, only you know how much you have contributed to this book. I love you very much.

iv

Part One
Coming Out

Introduction

I was an ex-convent schoolgirl turned lesbian activist, who simply didn't know how to come out to her mother.

My sexuality was integral to my work, and the activism that I was involved in was getting wide media coverage. It seemed as if I was out to the whole world, except my mother. It was time for desperate action.

For the last five years I have been one half of the two-woman theatre company 'Off-Limits'. So, deciding to use the medium I knew best, I set to work with my business partner, Sonya Braunton, and in conjunction with the director Jo Carter we devised a cabaret-style show for our next tour entitled, *There Must Be Fifty Ways To Tell Your Mother*.

We had obviously touched a nerve; from the first mail-out alone we got over forty bookings.

As we travelled around Britain, I realized that the show had a certain truthful quality. Lesbian and gay audiences were wincing in recognition within their laughter. The play seemed to be a trigger, and after the performance, in bars, cafes and car-parks, people began to tell me their stories.

The experiences I listened to were painful, funny, exhilarating and defiantly diverse; but somehow the show was having a unifying effect. The play was defining coming out as a rite of passage, and highlighting the fact that we share a common experience.

This book is about that experience, universal to every lesbian and gay man. Everybody has their own story, and I wanted to show the strength and wit that our community has developed as a coping mechanism.

Coming out is a continual process. Every day we have to keep taking the decision anew. Should I tell this person?

How? What will their reaction be? This book cannot provide answers, but offers the inspiration and ideas of others.

Men and women from all over the world are deciding to come out to their parents, their children, their employers and their partners. Here are some of their stories . . .

ABOUT THE BOOK

1. If a word is in **bold** you will find further details in the glossary at the back of the book.

2. Because many lesbian and gay people tend to move around, I have chosen to use their birthplace as a reference, unless they have expressly asked me not to.

CALL OUT

Yes, I'm down and feeling blue,
And I don't know what to do, so –
Ring, ring, why don't you give me a call?

ABBA

During your coming out process there will perhaps be times when you feel isolated and sad. The most important thing to remember is that you are definitely not alone. As you read through the stories in this book it will become apparent that others have shared your experiences.

Surveys have shown that perhaps one in every ten people is gay, however I think that two in every twenty sounds less lonely.

If you feel unable to talk to friends or acquaintances there are many switchboards that offer invaluable help and advice. You will find details of how to contact your local helpline in the glossary at the back of this book. Sometimes it is difficult to get through, but as the people below discovered, it is certainly worth persevering.

ANTHONY, ABERGAVENNY

I came out to myself when I was fifteen. I found the number of **Lesbian and Gay Switchboard** in the back of the *South Wales Argos*. I can remember the conversation so well. I feel like it's indelibly etched on my mind. I dialled, got through first time (unbelievably) but was too nervous to speak:

My Saviour: Hello, Lesbian and Gay Switchboard, how can I help you?

Me: (silence)

Him: I know you're there, I can hear you breathing.

Me: (silence)

Him: Well, my name is Mark.

Me: (silence)

Him: What's yours?

Me: Anthony.

Him: So why are you calling today, Anthony?

Me: Because I'm gay.

Him: What makes you think that?

Me: I really fancy men.

Him: Well, that's a good start . . .

And we worked on from there. It was fab.

Two years later, my mum found a letter I had been writing to my boyfriend. She read it, tutted, then said:

'All the time that you were failing exams, I thought it was because you were wasting time with girls. It turns out that you were wasting time with boys. I don't know.'

She told my dad while we were all watching *Shoestring*. He said (my dad that is, not Shoestring) that it was 'debased debauchery' and they took me to see a psychiatrist. This was a while ago, and I think I was very lucky to get the advice that I did. It could have been so very different. As it was, the psychiatrist said that it was my parents who had a problem, not me. They ignored this pronouncement, got angry, cried, and tried everything to make me realize the enormity of what I'd done. But I just pottered along, practising at being a poof.

Nowadays, my mum has got to the stage where she will say, 'Wish Claude [my current man] happy birthday from me.'

But it took ten years for them to realize that it wasn't a phase.

ALISTAIR, ISLE OF MAN

When I was fourteen, my mother asked me if I was gay. She was ironing at the time and I was just home from school. She seemed calm about it, she said, 'Watch out for old men,' and, 'You'll probably grow out of it.' I was very embarrassed as my family never discussed sex at all, and I ran up to my room.

I managed to get the number of the London Lesbian and Gay Switchboard and I phoned them. I couldn't believe that I was talking to a homosexual. When you're a child you have very strange ideas about what gay people are like and I was freaked out to be actually conversing with one. When I told him where I was calling from, he immediately realized that I had no outlet, nowhere to go for advice.

Being a gay teenager in the Isle of Man is a very negative experience. When I was at school, there was one gay pub in Douglas, which is the main town. I went there when I was sixteen, but it was a pretty nervous atmosphere. It got closed down by the police soon afterwards anyway, and then I had no outlet at all. As soon as I left school I went straight to London. I was desperate to come out.

The Isle of Man is a very incestuous community. I come from an old Manx background, so everyone knows you and your family. The pressure to conform is immense, and it is a totally closed system. You are related to most of the people around you, and whatever you do is public knowledge.

Although homosexuality was illegal at that time, there was a gay subculture, mostly involving married men. By the age of eighteen, I had slept with quite a few members of the government, all of them married men, and very sad men.

If I was straight I would go back home now. But as it is, I don't feel I can, even though the law has changed. That's a pity though, because the Isle of Man is such a beautiful place.

YAZ, AYR

It was Christmas Eve. Me and my mum were out delivering cards as she is too mean to buy stamps. She started talking about my brother and how she was hoping he would get a girlfriend. She was pleased because she thought that he had his eye on someone.

Suddenly, she turned to me and said, 'Have you ever had boyfriends? You never talk about them.'

I just replied, 'I don't think I will ever have a boyfriend actually.'

My mum looked puzzled and asked me what I meant by that. I was embarrassed and simply repeated that I would never have boyfriends, hoping that she would catch on. She didn't. She asked me why and I tried to make her guess. Eventually she said, 'Well I don't think you're a lesbian, if that's what you mean.'

'But that's exactly what I do mean,' I replied.

Unfortunately, at that moment we bumped into a friend of my mum's so we had to be all jolly and pretend that I hadn't just come out.

I was feeling upset and confused that night, so I decided to phone the switchboard. In Scotland it is only open three nights a week, but luckily that Christmas Eve was one of them. I had a phonecard which only had ten units on it, so I knew that I couldn't say very much. However, when I went into the phone box near my parents' house, I found a phonecard in there with fifty-four units on it. I felt as if fate was stepping in to help me. I phoned the switchboard who were so supportive and helpful that

I returned home feeling happy, and determined to try again with my mum.

Unfortunately, the conversation never got restarted, and the whole of Christmas passed without my mum or I referring to what had been said.

A few nights after Christmas though, my mum came into my room as I was going to sleep. She sat on the edge of the bed and told me that she hadn't slept for three nights. She said to me, 'The thing is, Yaz, I don't think you will ever be happy unless you marry and have children.'

I tried to reason with her, but she wasn't really listening to me. She came out with every cliché about lesbians that you can think of. Basically, we couldn't talk about it, and again the conversation was left unfinished.

I came out to my brother soon after this. He was very understanding and promised to try and talk to mum. I bought her a book called *A Stranger in the Family*, which is about coming to terms with having a gay child. I gave it to my brother to give to her. She read it and said that it helped her to understand what was going on.

My dad is Indian, and he would find it extremely difficult to accept my being a lesbian. I haven't told him yet, and my mum has asked me not to.

At college, I was one of the founder members of the lesbian, gay and bisexual society, which helped me to grow in confidence. I met a woman there on a demonstration. We got drunk together during the evening and ended up having sex in my room. That was when I knew I had come out to myself fully. I felt relieved. I got my hair cut in a mohican, which I might have done anyway, but I think that coming out has given me the confidence and courage to do so many things.

BOYS AND GIRLS COME OUT TO PLAY

Children are being taught that they have an inalienable right to be gay.

MARGARET THATCHER

The following section concerns people who knew that they were gay from an early age. As one young man I was interviewing put it: 'I knew I was a homosexual by the time I was eight, my treehouse had a breakfast bar.'

These stories contradict the homophobic theory that we 'choose' to become gay, in order to defy and irritate a straight world. If you come out to yourself during childhood, the process can be even more scary and traumatic. We need only look at statistics on lesbian and gay teenage suicide to realize that our young people are in desperate need of support mechanisms.

PETER, CHEAM

When I was eleven, I heard my parents talking about a toilet in the park where awful and disgusting things happened. So I got on my bike and went straight down there. I had sex with a man called Steve. He was at the **cottage** when I arrived. I told him that I was gay and asked if he was. He said, 'Yes,' and pulled me into a cubicle.

I loved every minute of it. He was the first person I told about my sexuality. Before that, I knew I liked men, but I didn't really know what sex was. I met Steve every Sunday, at three o'clock, until I was seventeen.

When I was fourteen, I wrote my mum and dad a letter. I think they knew I was gay because they kept asking me why I looked at men's groins. They are very traditional parents; my dad is a taxi driver and my mum stays at home and does all the house-work.

I wrote that I still loved them, but I couldn't lie to them about my sexuality. I also told them that I was having a relationship with Steve at the cottage. I gave them the letter one morning before I went to school. When I returned, they were throwing my things out of the bedroom window, shouting, 'You're not our son and we don't want you here any more.'

They had locked all the doors and I didn't know what to do, so I called the police, who contacted a social worker. Eventually, I went to a children's home. The other kids guessed my sexuality and I had to pretend that I had a girlfriend so they would leave me alone. I told the workers there that I was gay, but they said I was just after attention.

They sent me to a child psychologist called Dr Vasser. He was supposed to 'cure' me of my illness. He was convinced that I was straight and told my parents, so consequently they didn't believe anything I said. I continued that therapy for a year until Dr Vasser died. In the end I just used to laugh and muck around because I was so fed up with it all.

When I was sixteen, I heard about the **Albert Kennedy Trust**, and I applied to be fostered by two gay men. I contacted the Trust myself and four months later they found a couple for me to live with. I felt very relaxed living there and I met lots of other gay people. It is the best year that I can remember.

I am nineteen now and I always tell other people about the Albert Kennedy Trust so that they can get more gay carers.

Steve, the man from the cottage, caught HIV and died. He didn't know that you should use condoms during sex. If the edu-cation system wasn't so **homophobic** about sex lessons, I believe that he would be alive today.

9

MAXINE, PRESTON

I liked hanging around with older women; I was thirteen, they were sixteen. I was in the hockey team and I was a dyke. I didn't see it as a problem, but I knew I wasn't supposed to tell anyone. Society had already conditioned me. I was having sex with other girls in my class but we never talked about it.

I came out when we were having a family meal. I'd decided the time was right.

Me: You know my friend Samantha?

Mum: Pass the potatoes please, Maxine.

Me: Well, Samantha and I are both lesbians.

Mum: Oh, what does that mean?

Me: It means that we love each other and we have sex.

Mum: Oh.

Dad: Get out.

So I went upstairs, packed and left. It was New Year's Eve. I didn't speak to them for five years.

I got a job as a youth worker which I loved. There was one boy called Zeb. He was quite timid but aware. He didn't mix with the others much, he was a bit of a loner. We got on quite well though, and built up a friendship.

One particular day he seemed a bit preoccupied. He said that he wanted to ask me something.

Me: Feel free.

Zeb: Well, the thing is, are you a lesbian?

Me: Well, yes I am.

I knew why he was asking me and wondered whether he would be brave enough to come out with it. Unfortunately our conversation went no further. Two other young people had overheard and went running straight to the youth leader. I was immediately summoned to her office. She was terrified of **Clause 28** which had just been made law. She told me that I musn't 'promote' my sexuality, and I was suspended pending an enquiry.

As a last act of defiance I phoned my girlfriend and asked her to come and pick me up. I was waiting for her outside when Zeb appeared.

Zeb: Have I got you into trouble?

Me: No, it's not your fault.

Zeb: I didn't mean to cause problems.

Me: I know that.

Zeb: I just needed to tell you that I think I'm gay.

I gave him my home phone number which was probably highly unethical. I spoke to him a few times and he began attending a gay group in Brighton. He was fine. I got the sack. If I saw him now we'd probably have a laugh about it, but at the time it seemed dreadful. Lesbian and gay young people need just as much support as others, if not more.

I remember when I was first trying to come out, I saw a woman from school in the supermarket. I'd heard rumours about her and she certainly looked like a dyke.

I went up and started chatting, casually trying to steer the conversation round to the whereabouts of the nearest gay pub. She took me to the Queen's Arms in Brighton. I felt like I'd come home. These were people like me. It was a very affirming experience, a celebration of my sexuality and the most wonderful night of my life. I met a woman there and we went out together for two years.

My twin sister was married with four kids by the time I got around to coming out to her, so I guess that rubbishes the genetics argument.

I asked her to meet me and my partner in a quiet pub in Worthing. My sister appeared in the doorway and screeched across the room, 'I know you're going to tell me that you're a lesbian, Maxine.'

An old man at the bar choked on his pint. She advanced towards us. 'Is this your girlfriend, Maxine?' she yelled. 'Oh my God! She's wearing a skirt.'

11

My sister is not the most subtle person in the world. Every time I introduce her to a new girlfriend she says, 'Is this the one then?' I tell her that love's not like that. On the whole she's very supportive.

I think some of the family blamed me when my cousin came out. They said she was just copying me.

I recently called my mum. She said that she had missed me over the last five years but that it was water under the bridge. She didn't even know where I was living which made me feel a bit sad. We're beginning our relationship anew, taking it as it comes. At some stage I think we will need to discuss the past. But the time is not right yet.

She's been very helpful, giving me advice about my girlfriend's child. He has behavioural difficulties, like I did when I was younger. I guess you could say that the experience my mum gained bringing me up has really come full circle.

AAMIR, WIMBLEDON

I was having sex with men from quite a young age, about eleven I think. I knew that I wasn't interested in women and that I was different, but until I was about thirteen, I hadn't heard the word 'gay'. As soon as I did, and understood what it meant, I realized that it described me. It came as no big shock to me. It was like hearing the word 'Indian' for the first time.

I was having sex with men in public toilets, and I began quizzing them about their sexuality. I was intrigued. I'd have a quick bit of sex with them, then sit them down and say, 'Are you gay? Do you have a boyfriend? Tell me about your life.' Some of them were married, but most of them were quite happy to talk to me for a bit. Looking back, I was desperately trying to find out about gay people, and what being gay was about.

One day in the cottage I met a man called Martin. I didn't have any gay friends, but this man talked to me and connected with me. He even wanted to see me again. That was ten years ago. We've been together ever since.

FERNANDO, BARCELONA

I knew I was gay from the age of four. I remember the day so clearly because that morning at nursery school I'd done a very special drawing of a boat, and the nun had helped me write my name and age on it. I was so proud.

My elder brother came to pick me up and he took me down to the swimming pool. His friends were talking about how you got a hard-on if you managed to catch a glimpse of a girl in a bikini. A very rare sight in those days. I was listening and thinking how great it was to be allowed to hang out with such grown-up boys.

Then one of them said that if you got a hard-on when you saw a boy in his swimming trunks, you were a queer. They were all laughing but my blood froze. That was me. I knew, even at that age, that I fancied boys and somehow it was 'bad'. In bed that night I cried for a very long time but I couldn't tell anyone what was wrong. I just shut the knowledge away inside me.

When I got older I used to seduce the maid's children, but so did my brother, and he's now married with three kids. We used to French kiss, lots of kissing and playing with each other's genitals, but there was never any question of ejaculation.

At the age of eleven or twelve, I discovered the wonderful world of wanking. I used to feel very guilty about it though, and felt I was obliged to tell the priest the gory details at confession. Perhaps he got off on it because he never reprimanded me too severely. I never developed the savvy to realize that masturbating was OK. I just got fed up with confessing it every week.

Then I got sent to public school. I used to hang around with three other boys. We were known as 'the sisterhood'. Everyone knew we were gay, we knew we were gay, but we never talked about it. In my year of about a hundred boys, I reckon about thirty to forty were gay and that doesn't include the ones who had sex with boys on the side because there was no alternative.

My best friend in the sisterhood had four gay brothers, one of whom was a fashion student at St Martin's. We used to call him Auntie Ken, he was a real 1970s clone, and the first openly gay man that I ever remember meeting. He's probably dead now. Auntie Ken used to turn to us and say, 'At first children it's really painful, but after a while it's quite nice.' He was a wonderful and outrageous man.

I used to lie to my parents and tell them that I was far too busy to leave school on my weekends off. Then the sisterhood would travel to London and get taken to wild gay bars by Auntie Ken and his friends. It was mind-blowing for a fourteen-year-old.

It was around this time that my room-mate began to entertain me with unbelievable moonlit masturbatory rituals. He knew I was watching, but in the morning we had to pretend it just hadn't happened.

So in one way, sex was around, but I still felt very repressed because no one ever talked about it.

I knew I was definitely queer. I never felt sexually attracted to a woman. I used to dare myself to write it in the corner of my exercise books, very small, but perfectly legible. 'I'm gay.' But then I'd cross it out before anyone could see. In my secret journal I was writing as a gay man, and yet I wasn't out to anyone. I decided to tell my older brother.

I led into the conversation via some anecdotes about boys at school. I thought I was doing quite well when he suddenly stopped me: 'I hope you're not trying to tell me that you're gay because that would fucking kill me, and I will kill you.'

I was frightened and he was very angry. I couldn't believe the vehemence of his reaction. I just completely clammed up and was unable to mention it to him for years. This was one in a series of rejections I received from my family.

In the early 1980s, Hollywood attempted to talk about homosexuality through a film called *Making Love*. It was a bit naff but at least they were trying. Someone asked my father what he thought of this film. He looked directly at me as he said, 'I know that there is a problem with gay people. I suspect that they may need time and understanding. But I can't give them that and I don't care.'

He must have known, but was so unhappy about the situation that he never gave me or the subject any time. The nearest we ever got to a discussion was once when he picked me up at the end of term, and said, 'I have seen some of your friends at school and I'm deeply worried . . . you know what I'm talking about.'

He was waffling, but basically he was saying that if I dared to take this beyond a certain level there'd be trouble. I remember trying to summon up the courage to reply in a controlled tone of voice, 'You've got nothing to worry about. It won't affect you. I will not embarrass you.'

Instead of saying, 'we must talk about this,' he was practically saying, 'clam up now.' It was never mentioned again.

Throughout university I was going out with a man called Ben. I was crazily in love with him, I absolutely adored him. When he left me, I felt like my world was falling apart and I had a nervous breakdown. By the time I went to see my family, I weighed seven stone and was in a very bad way. But I was still not allowed to talk about what was wrong. I was terribly upset but they didn't want to hear why.

I decided I would not, and could not, collude with their self-deception any longer. I have not spoken to my parents for three years now. I will never have to formally come out to them because in my mind I consider them to be dead. Metaphorically killing them off was the only way I could survive.

I moved without informing them of my change of address.

However, last year, a letter arrived from my father. He must have used a private detective to track me down. This isn't unusual. I've known him use this method before.

Enclosed was an article about the demise of the family business. The accompanying note said: 'In spite of your gratuitous cruelty I thought you should read this.'

I don't think it is me who has been cruel.

I never replied.

TAM, CAMDEN

I knew I was a lesbian when I was quite small. I've never been interested in men. When I was eighteen I announced to my best friend that I had something important to tell her. She said, 'It's all right, I know that you're gay.' She was great. She was the first person I told.

My mum knows as well, because she read the love-letters from my girlfriend that were hidden in my room. She didn't let on straight away though. But one day while we were having an argument she suddenly shouted, 'At least I don't sleep with women.'

I didn't know whether to try and get out of it or just admit it. In the end I told the truth. She got really angry about it. She was brought up to believe that if you are gay you are completely mental, and should be locked up. She pushed me down the stairs and I was really scared. She couldn't look me in the face after that and the situation became unbearable. Six months later I moved out.

She doesn't want to know me as a daughter any more, she thinks I'm disgusting. We never see each other. It's a shame because I really miss my little brother.

MARTIN, PUTNEY

Although I knew I was gay from age eleven, I was married to

a woman, which isn't as much of a cop-out as it sounds. I was twenty-one in the year of the **Sexual Offences Act** (1967), and being gay was much more difficult then. I got married largely because I really liked the woman I was living with. It seemed the logical thing to do, and at that time I never believed I would meet a man who I wanted to share my life with. My wife knew the situation, I never pretended to be a straight man. We married because we were friends, and I continued to have sex with men.

A few years later, she got herself a lesbian lover who moved in with us. Shortly afterwards, I met the man of my dreams and fell completely in love. Strangely enough, I was still nervous about telling my wife. But meeting this man gave me the courage to accept my own sexuality fully, and I stopped worrying about other people finding out. We even started going around in a foursome; me and my wife, plus our gay lovers. People obviously assumed that we were two straight couples. But it was far more interesting than that.

STEWART, LANCASHIRE

I told my mum when I was sixteen. But the odd thing was, she said that I'd already told her when I was twelve. I have no recollection of doing this at all. Apparently, I was very upset at the time so I must have blocked it out. She seemed worried that if Gareth, my 'best friend', found out I was gay, he wouldn't come round any more and I would be lonely.

So I reassured her by telling her that Gareth definitely knew I was gay because he was my boyfriend. Then mum said that he couldn't come round any more, and so I *was* lonely. She said she didn't mind me having relationships with men, it's just that she didn't want me to have sex with them. Then about a month later she said, 'You're really mean, you haven't invited Gareth round for ages.' I guessed she'd come to terms with it.

My mum told me not to tell my dad. However, he must have

overheard some of the discussion because later he took me to one side and in an extraordinarily calm voice said, 'It's OK if you're gay. It's just that you must leave this house and never, ever come back again. Understand? So are you gay?' I denied it.

It was twelve years before I felt able to tell my dad the truth.

When I finally managed it, he was reasonable, saying it was just the dressing up he didn't understand. When I told him that I had no particular desire to dress like a woman, he seemed surprised. He thought that all gay men were into **transvestism**.

I recently went for a job interview. At the bottom of my CV it says, 'President of the LGB Society'. I hadn't felt brave enough to put, 'Lesbian, Gay and Bisexual'. My prospective employer seemed particularly pleased.

'That's a good sign, young man,' he said, beaming across the desk at me.

'It is, sir?' I replied, hopefully.

'Oh yes! I went to Lutterworth Grammar School for Boys myself . . .'

I didn't get the job.

STEVEN, NEWCASTLE

When I was eight, I had pictures of Tony Blackburn up by my bed. I used to cut them out of the *Radio Times*. He was a real fantasy figure in my life. At that age you obviously don't have the language to express sexual feelings, but there was a definite fascination there. It was around this time that I started a physical relationship with my friend Jonathan. It lasted for six years.

During this time – I must have been about eleven – I got seduced by a man of eighteen, Malcolm. It was wonderful, I absolutely loved it. The whole experience was totally fantastic and totally consensual. I rushed home afterwards and taught Jonathan everything I'd learnt.

However, the sad thing is that I didn't realize that we had

18

done anything 'wrong'. I was really innocent in this respect. I went around telling my friends and saying, 'Guess what I did the other day!'

Inevitably, I suppose, my parents found out, and Malcolm just vanished off the face of the earth. I never found out exactly what happened to him. I know you lack judgement at this age, but I'm sure he got into deep trouble.

I still worry about what happened, Malcolm was a very sweet man. We had shared this wonderful experience, but it was now soured with this abhorrent aftertaste. I feel guilty about what I did to Malcolm, but certainly not about what he did to me.

LUCY, MANCHESTER

I had a crush on Chris Evert, and Martina made me feel funny. It was 1979 and I was watching the women's final with my dad. My PE teacher had already told me that Chrissy should win because 'she was more representative of women's tennis', whatever that meant.

I can just remember that everyone had a vague, unfocused dislike of Martina, and I was totally on her side. This fascination is a very strong memory for me.

At the age of twelve or thirteen I can remember thinking that I might be gay, or at least bisexual. I would scour the *Guardian* women's pages, desperate for information to build up the half-image I had of this sexuality.

I never really dated men. I had a short affair with a boy called Brass, but we were both fourteen and it had no future.

When I was seventeen, I started going out with a girl who'd been to the same nursery school as me. Our parents were friends so it was very convenient. She was just dabbling really, but it was quite a positive experience for me. We began to explore what scene there was in Manchester at the time.

The sad thing is that I really regressed when I went to Oxford.

I was so ready to come out, but my whole experience there was so negative. During my first term I went to the introductory meeting of the lesbian and gay group, but that made me retreat even further back into the closet. The gay society seemed to consist of twenty-three very camp men and one horsy dyke. Where were all the lesbians? I checked out the women's group but they certainly weren't there. In retrospect, I think I should have looked in some of the women-only colleges, but you live and learn.

When I was twenty, I went to Europe with my best friend. We were sitting outside a cafe in Italy, a very cosmopolitan setting, and I said to her, 'Wouldn't it be awful if I was gay?'

You can tell I was feeling very positive about myself. She replied that it would be awful if I thought that I was and I wasn't, which isn't a terribly helpful answer. In fact, no one I can remember speaking to at this time was really helpful.

I think it's terrible that there is no support service at Oxford. It makes me very angry. Perhaps things are better nowadays, but I doubt it.

Eventually I went to see one of my tutors, who asked me what experience I'd had and didn't seem very impressed by my one adolescent relationship. Her advice, which I dutifully followed, was to go and read **Oranges Are Not The Only Fruit**. I found this book completely inspirational, and was delighted when she offered to introduce me to Jeanette Winterson.

However, a couple of days before the planned meeting, I found a note in my pigeon-hole, cancelling. My tutor had decided that Jeanette was too much of an unpractical theorist to be of any real help.

I realized that the only way I was going to move forward was if I bit the bullet myself. I chose a friend at college and simply told him, 'I'm gay.' I don't think he realized how important his positive reaction was to me. In coming out to him I think I was finally coming out to myself.

I told my sister, and her response was very reassuring. She said that it made much more sense of me. Her acceptance has cemented our relationship.

I decided to take a year off university to get myself sorted out and hopefully have some fun. I went home for a week and broke both my pieces of news. My dad choked on his tea and told me, 'Don't forget that you can think one thing and do another.'

My mum got a bit tearful and said that it was sad that I wouldn't be able to have any children, and then continued, 'And you were always so fond of your father.' What relevance that has, I still haven't fathomed. They were both quite perplexed, 'But you've always been so feminine.'

Somehow my lesbianism combined with a year off was seen as a general descent into delinquency. Not to mention the fact that I'd taken to wearing overcoats. They both blamed the fact that I'd been reading a lot of Virginia Woolf and thought that somehow she'd managed to seduce me – if only.

I went back to Oxford and began sleeping with women, though not really having relationships.

I remember seeing a documentary on Channel 4 at this time called *Veronica 4 Rose*. It was a real epiphany for me. I couldn't believe that there were real-life lesbians on TV. It was very empowering. I thought, 'That's me.'

My parents gradually got used to the idea, and told one of their friends. Her theory was that intellectual women were often lesbians. I think her acceptance helped my parents. Since I've been in a settled relationship my parents have been great. I think they presumed that I was going to be a sad spinster living as a recluse, and they were relieved to see me in a happy partnership. Nowadays, the postcards come addressed to both of us.

I'm not out to my other relatives. I think my parents use my intelligence to counter questions about my sexuality. I'd find it very hard to come out to someone from my grandparents' generation. However, the other day my granny said, 'Our Lucy's not boy-minded.' I wonder if she knows how right she is.

FISCH, LONDON

My parents split up when I was thirteen. My mum moved away and I stayed with my dad for a while. I knew I was attracted to girls even then, but we never discussed it. At fifteen, by which time I was a fully-fledged lesbian, I went to live with my mum. I pretended to go out with boys, despite never feeling right about it.

When I got a girlfriend and took her home, my mum flipped. She said, 'I know you're a lesbian, but I don't want it under my roof.' We both left immediately, and my mum and I didn't speak for ten years.

Two years ago I made contact with her hoping she had come to terms with it. She hadn't changed at all, and still didn't want to know about my sexuality. She died soon after.

A FAMILY OUTING

It's a family affair.

SLY AND THE FAMILY STONE

The people in this chapter have all discovered that one of their relations shares their sexuality. Thinking about it, the possibilities are endless: marching with your mum, cruising with your cousin, dancing the night away with dad. So next time you're at that family gathering, check out the vibes, you never know who you might discover . . .

JOSEPH, YORKSHIRE

Me and my brother Christian always knew that we were both gay. We just never spoke about it. I had a girlfriend for six years though, called Tina, and we had a brilliant sex life. Making love to her at night was like having cocoa. It was my nightcap. I loved it. I told Tina when we were very young that I was gay, but we didn't speak about it. I didn't lie to her though, and I never messed around with anyone else. I wouldn't have dreamt of it. I loved her, she was fab. She was my soulmate. We're close friends now and I'm still wild about her. She's as camp as hell.

My brother had a girlfriend too, called Lisa. Lisa used to sit on his face and say, 'If you don't lick it, I'll tell everyone that you're gay.'

He regrets it now and wishes that he had the courage to stand up for himself. But I think it's great that we've both enjoyed women as well as men.

I went to work abroad, and while I was there I phoned Christian and told him that I was gay. He seemed quite freaked out, but said that he accepted it. I returned to England, and Christian went off to Mexico where he phoned me and told me exactly the same thing.

It seemed quite strange at first but we felt such unity between the two of us. Soon after that, Christian went to mum and told her that he was gay. She took it well. But when I told her that I was too, she said, 'Don't be stupid, you're just trying to copy Christian.' I pleaded with her to believe me but she was sure I would grow out of it.

She still doesn't accept it completely, probably because she saw me with Tina for so long. Christian takes boyfriends home, but I don't have the courage to do that. I know she wouldn't take it seriously. However, if I meet someone special and have a serious relationship, I will definitely take him back.

I come from a theatrical family. My mum is a cross between

23

Dolly Parton and Lily Savage, so to come out to a mother like that isn't very hard. The only really negative reaction I have had from family was my sister-in-law. She came to stay with me and brought her own sheets. She also said, 'My children must never know.' She's such a naff woman though, I just laughed at her.

ISLA, LONDON

My mother is bisexual, and came out to me when I was about four by introducing me to her girlfriend. I came out to her about three years ago. She asked what had taken me so long. We're the best of friends now, she babysits for me a lot.

My dad is as straight as they come, and he hasn't spoken to me since he discovered that I'm a lesbian. It's his loss.

PERRY, FARNHAM

I was fifteen and I was sitting on the pavement outside a pub. My cousin, Amina, told me that she was gay, and I said, 'That makes two of us.'

She was delighted, and I was in a state of shock that I'd actually said it. Amina whisked me off to **Heaven** straight away. And they let me in! It nearly blew my mind; just hundreds of gay people. Up until then I thought I was the only one. In fact, I hadn't really thought I was gay. Just that I fancied blokes. At fourteen, I had snogged another man, and I wasn't even really out to myself. But I remember him playing with my hair and it being electric and very exciting.

When my cousin Amina had said, 'You're gay!' it was the first time someone had called me that without it being an insult. At school it was always an insult. The words had such negative connotations. At fifteen I remember thinking, 'But I still want to get married and have children.' Four years on I don't worry about that any more.

That very first night in Heaven, there was a guy nearby. In fact there were several hundred! But this particular man was a very good dancer. He was about forty or fifty. Amina said, 'Look, there's something to celebrate. You wouldn't be doing that at his age if you were straight.'

At the moment I can't really conceive of telling my parents. I think my dad might feel physically sick. When I was young, I had loads of girlfriends, and my mum used to say, 'I'm glad you're That Way and not the Other Way.'

I wouldn't tell them unless I had someone specific to tell them about. If my mum asked me, I'd tell her, otherwise I'd miss my big chance. Also, I presume that if your parents ask you, it means they've been thinking about it, and are probably ready to listen. I'd really like to tell my sister, but it's getting harder because her lifestyle just seems so conventional.

I am happy, but I feel like I'm living a lie. I find it very difficult to come out to straight men. I think that maybe they'll feel threatened, so I protect them. Whereas I find it really easy to tell girls.

Perhaps my sister knows already, because once she opened my photographs before I did. Normally I censor them before public viewing. There was a picture of me snogging my boyfriend, but she never mentioned it. So neither did I.

BECKY, KENDAL

I was seventeen and involved in my local **CND** group. They had lots of meetings and discussions, but rarely did anything. I was bored with it. I had boyfriends but I wasn't very impressed with that either. I thought there was something wrong with me because I didn't like sex, but my mother assured me that it got better.

At one point I thought, 'Am I queer?' I didn't want to be, so I decided I could pretend to be straight. I lived in a tiny community and I didn't know anyone who was gay.

My mum was very open about sex and knew that I was sleeping with boys when I was sixteen. We always talked about personal issues, and I knew that I could turn to her if necessary.

Through the CND group I heard about an action at **Greenham Common** and decided to go. When I arrived, I was completely entranced by it all and saw my chance to get involved in something. I just remember images of hundreds of women and lots of mud.

Soon after that first visit, I decided I wanted to return, so my mother drove me down and left me there. Instead of going back to sixth form I began living at Greenham.

My mother was unsure at first, but eventually she came round and even helped me build a shelter to live in. There were lots of dykes there and I got involved with another sixteen-year-old. It was great for us being in such a positive lesbian environment. I was nervous about telling my mother, but she had read all the gossip about lesbians at Greenham so eventually she asked me. Her experiences with men had been so bad that she couldn't really condemn my relationship. She accepted it and never made me feel weird about it.

A year later, my mum moved to Greenham as well and started having a relationship with a woman. Initially I thought she was cramping my style, but in the end we got on fine. We were together there for about two years.

My mother's stance is that everyone is bisexual and she has been able to express both sides of her sexuality. Personally I think she prefers women though.

DAVE, PERTH

I was in the pub with my brother, Brian, and we were being 'laddie'. I was trying to come out to him, and he was laughing because he knew what I was going to say. So I said it, and he laughed even more. He said that it wasn't such a big deal, and that he'd had sex with loads of his building-site friends. In fact, once he'd been fucking a guy over the arm of the sofa while my nan was in the bath upstairs. We started telling outrageous stories, seeing who could outdo the other. The people in the pub were probably fascinated. I made a joke that it was all his fault anyway, because he'd made me suck him off in a tent in the back garden when I was eleven.

I wasn't shocked when my brother started telling me about his sex with boys, even though he is married with two kids. Once, when I was about seven or eight, we'd invited lots of friends over to stay the night because it was my brother's birthday. Loads of people were sleeping on our bedroom floor. I remember waking up in the middle of the night, and there was a big '**daisy chain**' of boys all fucking and sucking. I couldn't believe my eyes. It was so exciting. But I had to keep still in case they realized I was awake and stopped what they were doing. Luckily, most of them seemed pretty engrossed. I was so jealous, I wanted to join in, but I knew they thought I was too young to play with them, so to speak.

I think that my brother must be bisexual. Sometimes he seems jealous of the sexual freedom that I have in my life, but he does love his children very much. Brian says that his wife knew he used to sleep with his friends sometimes, and she used to turn a blind eye.

I suppose in a way we both came out that night. It made it very easy for me to talk, knowing that Brian couldn't possibly disapprove of what I was saying.

Our mum has always encouraged us to be open about sex and ask her questions. But I know she never meant gay sex. Can you imagine? 'Mum, do you think it's safe to swallow?'

I think that maybe, deep down, she does know about me, but she doesn't want her suspicions confirmed. Neither of us want our relationship to be disturbed. We're scared of destroying what we've got. And as for Brian, he says he doesn't have men any more. But I'm not sure if I believe him.

OUTSTANDING PARENTS

It's one life, and there's no return and no deposit,
One life, so it's time to open up the closet.
Your life is a sham till you can shout out
I am what I am.

LA CAGE AUX FOLLES

There is a scene in the play/film *Steel Magnolias* when we hear how the gay character (he's obviously queer because his living room has spotlights) came out to his parents by basically saying: 'Hey, mom, dad, I've got terminal cancer. No, actually I'm joking. But I am gay.'

This bizarre vignette is struggling to make a valid observation. It is vital to remember that 'I'm gay' is never the worst thing we can say.

Perhaps we should also endeavour not to underestimate our parents. Sometimes they can surprise us with their reactions . . .

ZOE, LONDON

When I was nineteen, I was about to move in with my girlfriend, so I thought I should tell my mother. I remember it as a very teary evening. The conversation went something like this:

Me: (in between sobs) Mum, I'm a lesbian.

Mum: Oh good! I thought you were pregnant.

Me: You're pleased?

Mum: Ooh yes. Men are such bastards. I think my ideal would be a woman with a dick . . .

It was a very bonding experience. Mum told me that she'd had sex with a woman, but she wouldn't tell me who.

I was drunk when I came out to my ten-year-old sister. She obviously feared the worst:

Sis: You're not going to tell me about periods again are you?

Me: No, but I am a lesbian.

Sis: (tutting) God! Is that all? I knew that.

My dad just seemed pleased that he wouldn't have to shell out on some huge wedding.

MADELAINE, LIVERPOOL

I was going to the *Rocky Horror Show* with a transvestite friend. It was the social event of the year and my excitement level was high, but I remember being nervous in case my dad found out where I was going.

I made elaborate preparations involving complicated excuses, and snook out of the house with my costume stuffed into the bottom of my handbag. It's lucky you're not supposed to wear very much.

I got dressed into my very creased outfit in the toilets at the bus station – very glamorous. I made it to the theatre just in time, and as I walked into the auditorium I saw my dad in the audience right in front of me. He was in full drag.

JACKIE, BRISTOL

I'd gone home specifically to tell my mum. All weekend I'd been trying – and failing. On the Sunday evening mum took me to the station. I got on the train and was hanging out of the window, mum was on the platform. I suddenly decided to tell her, so I blurted it out. She calmly replied, 'I've always wondered about your grandmother, and as for myself, if I'd ever had the chance . . .'

At that exact moment the train pulled out. We've never mentioned it since.

ZOE, LONDON

I think that my eleven-year-old brother might be gay. My mum told me he was having problems at school. I said that I remembered going through similar unhappiness, and suggested that perhaps he was wrestling with his sexuality too. She seemed angry and told me not to 'tar everyone with my brush'. She said it would be statistically unfair if she had two gay children. Mum's not as liberal as she thinks she is.

JO, HERTFORDSHIRE

I actually told my mother I was a lesbian three months ago, but in fact she had known for about four years. I accepted that I was gay after I had my first lesbian relationship six years ago, but I didn't tell mum because she would have been too upset.

I wasn't keen to come out to the rest of my family as one of my sisters is very **homophobic** and I didn't want to cause friction. In the end, I couldn't keep it to myself any longer, so I phoned up the family one by one and told all of them the same night. My mum was really cool about it. I just said to her, 'I'm coming to see you and I'm bringing my girlfriend with me.'

She didn't bat an eyelid. She just asked me her name and said that it was fine. I was shocked at myself for being so direct, but I hadn't planned it that way. She phoned me back half an hour later and told me that she had known for four years and had expected me to tell her sooner or later.

So I took Rachel home to meet my mother and it all went remarkably well. My mum took me aside at one point and said, 'Are you happy now? Are you sure this is what you want?'

I told her it was.

My mother says that I've always been 'a bit of a feminist', and this is what made her think I was a lesbian. Also, I never had boyfriends while my sisters were in long-term relationships with men. When I became Women's Officer at college, she knew for sure.

There is a policy in my family that nobody talks about sex. We never got the facts-of-life lessons from our parents, and certainly no one discusses their own sex life. It is probably because of this that I kept it quiet for so long. I was never asked if I was seeing anybody because my family don't ask such questions.

The night of the coming out phone calls, the only person I didn't phone was my homophobic sister. My mum was annoyed about this, but I just couldn't face the first wave of abuse. I still haven't told her to this day. She knows though. She told my mum it was disgusting.

My dad was a bit of a different story. My parents split up just after Rachel and I started living together. He had nowhere to go, so he came to stay with us and the couple we shared with. I hadn't come out to him at that point, but he was completely laid back about it. He knew we slept together but didn't seem perturbed by it. In fact, he never asked about it.

Coming out to your family is such a release. You can be open about your life and share things that you previously kept a secret. Anything is possible – look at my dad. He's now happily living with four lesbians.

SEAN, SUNDERLAND

I'm very lucky, my mum and dad were marvellous. Even though my dad had a very smug look on his face. I think he must have known already. He was almost overly understanding, saying that he presumed now I'd come out, he would hear less about 'Dominique' my new friend, and more about 'Dominic'.

I then had to 'come out' all over again. This time for Dominique, clarifying her identity as my new female friend, and not my first boyfriend. My dad seemed almost disappointed.

JEMIMAH, LIVERPOOL

I told my mum and she was great, very accepting. In fact, the next time me and my girlfriend went to visit my parents, she put us in a double bed in the guest room. She said she'd discussed the matter with my dad, and even though she hadn't gone into specifics, he seemed fine about the situation. But I'm not sure her generalizations had successfully outed me to my dad. Later that evening, as we were getting ready for bed, he knocked, and put his head round the door.

'Now you girls, go straight to sleep. No whispering and giggling, and don't be staying up half the night having midnight feasts. You'll only get biscuit crumbs in the bed.'

The last time we'd had this sort of conversation I'd been twelve, and had a friend staying the night for a treat. I was now twenty-seven. Well, we did feast for half the night, nibbling and sucking on all sorts of delicious morsels. But not a biscuit crumb in sight.

MELANIE, WOLVERHAMPTON

I think my mum was haunted for years by the programme about a woman from South Dakota, whose six daughters all turned out to be dykes. When I came out to her, she immediately phoned my brother and sister and made them come out as heterosexual, 'just to be sure how many I've got to get used to'.

SUZANNE, AUSTRALIA

I told my mum I was gay when I was twenty-five, but I think she knew already. Every time we passed the local gay bar she would say, 'I bet you go there.' I used to get really uptight about it.

One day I took her out to lunch. Straight away she knew that I had something to tell her. When I finally revealed that I was a lesbian, thinking she wouldn't be surprised, she just said, 'No you're not actually. I've already thought about this. You've got a hormone disorder.' And she just carried on eating. This, I suppose, was the kind of reaction you'd expect from someone who lives in the middle of the desert. Then she tried to change the subject but I wouldn't let her.

'Why don't you talk to Auntie Helen?' I suggested, 'Her daughter's a dyke too.' My mother failed to respond. Eventually I started giggling and we finished the meal without speaking.

She did eventually come to terms with it though, and three years later, I was able to take my girlfriend home for the first time. My mother bought her a Christmas present and forced my grandmother to do the same. Mum was really terrific about my partner being there. We could cuddle in the house and everything! She still thinks I've got a hormone disorder though.

OUT OF YOUR CONTROL

Maybe a great magnet pulls all souls towards the truth.

K.D. LANG

You're trying to work out how to tell them . . .

The search is on for the ideal location, the perfect time, that special outfit. Jump-suits are not recommended for either sex at this juncture.

You're beginning to think it will never happen, when . . . *they ask you*! Is it a relief, or do you feel that your moment was usurped?

SARAH, WORTHING

I was on the phone to my mum and she said, 'I suppose you're going to tell me that you're a lesbian, aren't you?'

So I just said, 'Yes.' I was relieved, but freaked out. It hadn't crossed my mind that she had any idea. I got off lightly really. It was very easy for me. I was ill at the time, with anorexia, and I think this helped me to 'get away with it'. It somehow put my sexuality into perspective. What my mum wanted most was for me to get better, and my being a lesbian seemed suddenly less important.

The harder bit for me was trying to get her to fully accept it and talk about it, to ask me questions about my life without being scared of the answers. I think she believes that I became a lesbian as a result of hanging around with too many gay men, and because I had a bad time with a man when I was younger. She thinks that it's your life experience that makes you gay, not that you're born that way, or rather this way.

I never told my dad, although obviously my mum did. He says things like, 'I'm glad you're happy,' but we'd never talk about the issue directly.

LEE, CHINGFORD

My mother knows that I'm gay, in fact she was the first person to find out. I liked boys when I was a kid, but I used to read Enid Blyton books so I thought the word 'gay' meant happy. I was scared when I first realized that I was a homosexual, I didn't want to be. I started going out with girls, and eventually got engaged. A few weeks before the wedding my fiancée broke it all off. I was secretly relieved as I didn't really know why I was doing it anyway.

A short time afterwards, my mum noticed a huge lovebite on my neck. She said, 'Who gave you that, a man or a woman?' I just froze. I didn't know what to say, so I made an excuse to leave, and went back to my flat.

An hour later she phoned me. We had a long chat during which she said, 'Are you gay? It doesn't matter if you are, you know.'

'So what if I am?' I replied.

There was a long silence, then she said that it didn't change a thing and I was still her son. Then I got the safe-sex lecture and she told me that she had known for years. Since that day we have become really close, so coming out was a positive thing for me.

My nan came down last Christmas and I decided to tell her too. She is a pretty formidable woman, and being quite old, I didn't want to upset or shock her too much. I picked my moment and just came out with it: 'Nan, I'm gay.'

She said that she already knew and could have told me that herself when I was six. So much for her being shocked. I was stunned.

My friend, who is eighteen, has AIDS. He has been given less than two years to live. When I heard, I went home and cried all day. That could be me.

BETH, WALES

I didn't choose to come out, the whole situation just happened. I had a stupid argument with my parents and shut myself in my room. A few minutes later they were banging on the door saying, 'We know why you're behaving like this. You're queer, aren't you?'

I thought, 'This is brilliant. At last we are going to discuss it.' So I simply said, 'Yes, I am.' My mum left the room and was physically sick.

My dad went mad. He grabbed a Stanley knife off my desk and said he was going to kill the person I was going out with. I tried to point out that I didn't think this was a very good idea. Seconds later my dad had me pushed up against the wall, knife at my throat. His exact words were, 'I would rather see you dead than queer. Make your choice.'

In situations like this, you realize that there is a time to fight the cause and a time to stay alive.

I told him it wasn't true and that I'd never had sex with a woman. He got a bible from the bookshelf and made me swear that I wouldn't even contemplate going out with a woman in the future. The whole incident was getting out of hand, so I promised. He said we'd never mention it again.

One week later, I was staying overnight with my friend, a well-known heterosexual. At midnight the phone rang. I was urgently summoned home. My mum had broken into my room, searched it, and found all my old diaries and letters. As I walked into the house, I could see them spread out on the living-room floor. She made me sit while she read bits out to me.

Basically, she believed that I'd never had sex with a woman. These personal papers showed that I had, more than once. She was disgusted. Perversely, my dad would not get involved. He said that he trusted me to keep to the agreement that we had made. He referred to it as some kind of legally binding contract. He said the past didn't matter.

My mother made me rip up every single letter, card and photograph. Later, when she was calmer, she told me that many women had these unnatural feelings and the decent thing to do was just to get on with your life. She said that, despite these thoughts, it was possible for me to meet a nice man, marry, and have a normal home with children. I had the unnerving feeling that she was talking from experience.

Nowadays we never mention it. I think that my father believes he made me renounce my evil ways. I suspect that deep down, my mother knows that I still feel the same, but she never brings the subject up.

In four years' time my youngest sister will be sixteen. I may well confront my parents about my sexuality then. I won't at the moment, because I'm scared that they'll stop me seeing my sister. When she's sixteen she can decide for herself.

My other sister is very supportive, but she's bisexual so we can share girlfriend tips. I told her that I was gay when I was twelve or thirteen. She said she knew anyway. I suppose the Madonna pictures were a bit of a give-away. Also I was in love with my best friend which was a big clue.

My partner is very sympathetic about my situation, she understands how difficult it can be. She's eighteen years older than me and not out to her own parents. We have a wonderful relationship. Last year we had a pretend Christmas, three days before the actual event: presents, dinner, the full works. It was great.

I've got a flat across the road from her house. Basically I live with her, but the flat gives me somewhere to stay when her parents come visiting. She introduced me to her mum and dad last time, just as a friend, but I was glad to meet them.

My nightmare scenario would be my father finding out that I am involved in a lesbian relationship with an older woman, and coming round to her house. I'm not so scared of his violence towards me, but I couldn't bear it if he laid a finger on my partner.

I do feel very angry when I think about the past and I would like my work to help others feel less intimidated. Sometimes I think I'll travel to India or Bangladesh and help women there who have absolutely no freedom. However, I know that there is just as much I could do for people closer to home. I'd like to have an educational position to be able to show people that their choices need not be restricted.

Over the last year I've been working with the students' union at college, but I come into contact with quite a narrow cross-section of people: on the whole, white, middle-class women who haven't had much experience of their own oppression. They are the beautiful people. There are many other groups of women who get forgotten about.

I'm very out at work. I think it's extraordinarily important. You never know what hope you might be bringing to others by being so visible. There is a lot of institutionalized homophobia at my college, and I've found the NUS [National Union of Students] quite positive and helpful as I've tried to tackle this. Also, the rest of the Student Union executives have always been amazingly supportive. They've never made me feel like I'm standing alone facing hostility.

I'm sure that some of the students have bitched behind my back, I've felt really negative vibes at times. But I think my attitude has confounded the critics. Their back-biting euphemisms – 'mad, ranting feminist' etc. – ring hollow when I'm being my friendly, good-natured, charming self.

Perhaps the most depressing aspect is that most students are too self-centred to care whether their union members are gay, straight or whatever. In the recent student union elections only 900 out of a possible 10,000 voted. The level of apathy is stunning. They have choice and they don't use it. You only realize how precious that is when it's taken away.

PATRICK, BOURNEMOUTH

The first person I came out to was my best friend Vanessa, just before we went to university together. She made some comment about finding me a girlfriend, and I piped up: 'Actually, I think you'd better find me a boyfriend.'

For some reason she was completely surprised, God knows why, the woman had known me for two years. Vanessa was a terribly right-on person who was always complaining that none of her friends were gay. So she thought it was fab. She did tell me though that I would have to get in shape. 'Gay men are very choosy,' she warned, 'very selective. So if you want to get a boyfriend, get some muscles.'

At the age of twenty, while at university, I did have a boyfriend. I decided, therefore, that it was time to tell my mum and dad that I was gay. I warned my boyfriend Alex that I planned to tell them at Christmas and would probably need a lot of support afterwards.

When my mum picked me up in the car, she started asking lots of questions about college. She asked me if I was seeing anyone, and when I blushed she started pursuing the point. She started asking what my girlfriend's name was, what she was like and so on, while I just continued blushing. Then there was a pause and she said, 'Or is it a boy that you're going out with?' I turned off the Erasure tape we were playing and answered, 'No, it's a man actually and his name is Alex.'

I told her I had always known I was gay, that I was happy, and very pleased to be going out with this man (not realizing what a wanker he was at the time). My mother cried all the way home, which I found a bit stressful, so when we got back I went out for a walk. I decided to phone my ever-trustworthy boyfriend Alex, only to discover he had unplugged his phone for three days.

Anyway, my mum and I decided not to tell anyone else in the family; my dad because he would have a bad reaction, and my brother because he was a butch rugby-playing sort of guy. However, the next time I talked to my brother on the phone, we were discussing Christmas presents. I was wittering on about what I'd seen in Habitat when he suddenly said, 'Patrick, I know.'

It turned out my mum had told his girlfriend who in turn had told him. But he was fine. He said to me, 'Patrick, you're my brother, I love you, I want you to be happy.' Apparently, he'd found some porno mags of mine months before, and had been waiting ever since for me to come out to him.

But as for Alex, when I finally got hold of him and told him my story, he chucked me. That was the day before my twenty-first birthday. So that was my boyfriend, a good-looking man, just slightly dysfunctional!

ANYA, CARDIFF

The day I left home I was eighteen. My mum shouted after me as I walked down the path, 'Don't drink, don't smoke, and don't go with any girls.'

I guess she must have had her suspicions about me being a dyke even then. As the years went by I just reinforced her ideas. I was always dropping my girlfriend's name into the conversation, and producing her at various family gatherings. Eventually my mother had to accept that I did 'go with girls'.

Her concern then seemed to be the number of girls I 'went with'. Was I in fact a bit of a goer? She voiced this concern to me by the frozen meat counter in Marks and Spencers one day:

Mum: You don't go with other girls besides Gina, do you?

Me: It's all right, mum, I'm in a long-term monogamous relationship.

Mum: That's all very well, but do you sleep with other girls?

I reassured her that I didn't, and told her that lesbians were amongst the people least likely to get HIV. She asked me not to go into details. Her knowledge in this area has always been a bit dodgy. She once told me you could get AIDS from a toilet seat.

KATHLEEN, ALASKA

I came out as bisexual to my mother about three years ago. At the time, that's what I thought I was, and I was very strongly involved in bisexual politics. When I told her, we were in the middle of a telephone conversation. The first thing she said was, 'Do you realise that you can get AIDS from women too?'

She thought that it was 'abnormal', she kept using that word. I told her that it was her fucking problem if she thought that, and I slammed the receiver down. Luckily she phoned back the next day.

It's kind of ironic, because I'd always said that being 'bi' wasn't a phase, but as time went on I realized that in my case it was.

I know that it's totally different for other people, but I just had to accept that I was definitely a lesbian now. However, for some strange reason I found this more difficult to explain to my mom.

The next time I saw her, she asked me if I had been going out with any boys. I told her that I hadn't dated men for three years. She then said, 'Well, I don't believe in bisexuality, so if you're a lesbian why don't you just come out and say so?'

I didn't answer her at first. Then I asked if she would accept me with a female partner and she said that she would probably have to at some point. I didn't feel that this was a very positive response.

After this, she kept bringing the subject up whenever we were alone, but she couldn't look me in the eye. I think it's easier to come out if you are actually dating someone, it somehow solidifies the rather abstract concepts that you are trying to explain.

Nowadays, she won't talk about it and never asks me if I am seeing anyone, or who I spend Christmas with. I get quite upset if I think about it too much. I do want to be fully out to my Mom, so I shall probably try again next time I see her.

DAMIEN, MALTA

I suppose I had it quite easy really. One day my mum just yelled from the kitchen, 'Damien, are you a poofter?' I said I was and we went on from there.

I blame her sudden awareness of the issue on the Oprah Winfrey show. They'd been 'doing' lesbianism a few days before. Oprah has got a lot to answer for.

LOLA, MASSACHUSETTS

All through high school I knew I liked women. I hated football matches but I used to go just to watch the cheerleaders. I was too shy to speak but I wanted them to like me, so at half time I took them marijuana joints. I didn't realize it was a sexual thing though.

I went to college away from home and started sleeping with this girl. Every time I came home, I kept wanting to tell my mum I was gay, because we were really close. I was constantly building up to it, then losing my nerve at the last moment. I knew she wasn't going to be that weird about it, but somehow I just never got it into the conversation.

After I split up with my first love, my mum noticed that something was wrong. One day she said to me, 'You seem very upset about something, are you gay?' I told her I was and I had been wanting to tell her. She said that as long as I was happy, it was OK.

When I was little, I remember driving past the school playground and being fascinated by the grown-up girls in their knee-high socks. I asked my mum if it was OK to look at girls. She replied, 'Yes of course, why do you think people buy women's magazines?' After that I just assumed that there was nothing wrong with it.

OUTED?

**Listen, do you want to know a secret,
do you promise not to tell?**

THE BEATLES

Even if you do manage to come out in your own time, sometimes the information is not treated with as much care as you might hope . . .

MICHAEL, LONDON

When I was twenty, my best friend was a gay woman called Georgie. She was the first person I came out to. I was a hairdresser and I used to cut her hair. Everyone at work knew that she had a girlfriend and they used to gossip about her a lot.

One night we went out for a drink, and she started talking about her girlfriend and relationships in general. She asked if I would ever consider sleeping with a man, and what I thought about homosexuality. I said that I didn't mind it, but that it wasn't for me. In fact, I went a bit overboard emphasizing that I would never, under any circumstances, sleep with a man. I think she was suspicious.

The next time we went out I decided to tell her that actually I didn't think it was that bad and I might quite like to try it (though secretly I already had, a couple of times).

I said to her, 'Look, I think I might be gay.' Georgie pretended that she hadn't guessed all along, and acted surprised. It was quite funny really.

After that I just started coming out to the world. I told everyone at work in one day. Then I thought about my family. I have a brother and a sister, both of whom are very heterosexual. When we were kids, my brother always wanted things like screwdrivers and bricks. I wanted things like dancing lessons. Anyway, after coming out to Georgie, I finished with my girlfriend, went to stay with Georgie, and decided to tell my mum.

I was perming my mum's hair one day, and she asked me why I had finished with my girlfriend. I was standing behind her putting the rollers in so she couldn't see my face. Actually, I think my mum knew what was coming because I had dyed my hair blond that week. I told her that the relationship just wasn't right and she accepted that. There was a silence and then I said, 'No, there's something I want to tell you, but I just can't say it.'

My mum got me some wine out of the fridge and I drank it while doing her hair, to give me courage. Then we sat down together and I said, 'Look, the reason I'm not going out with my girlfriend any more is because, er . . . because . . . er . . . I can't say it.'

My mum kept encouraging me, 'Just say it, I'm your mum anyway, it doesn't matter what it is,' but I couldn't say the word. In the end I said, 'The reason I'm living with Georgie at the moment is that she can help me with this thing because she knows all about it.' And my mum said, 'Are you gay?'

I blurted out, 'Yes I am,' and burst into tears, so my mum burst into tears too. She said that she knew anyway, but that she wanted me to tell her. So then it all came out about me wanting dance lessons and we talked for ages.

Almost immediately, my mum went really over the top and decided that everyone should know, because she said I had been in the closet too long.

The following Sunday, my sister's baby was being christened, and the whole family was round our house. My mum got us all into one room and said, 'OK everyone, there's an announcement I have to make.' I was hoping that it wasn't what I was thinking. It was. When everyone was quiet, she continued, 'Right, Michael and I had a chat yesterday and he's told me that he's a homosexual, so if anyone's got any problems I'd like it said. I don't want any gossiping.' I was burning with embarrassment. I was like Joan of Arc. Consequently, everyone started being ridiculously nice, saying, 'Ah! Are you? Ahh! I always thought you were.'

After that, the christening was completely forgotten, and it became my coming out party. It was really good. I came out in one big boom.

My dad wasn't too good about it at first. He said that I couldn't be gay because I came from a family of straight people. He must have thought that it was inherited: that two gay people got together to make a gay baby. Also, when I first came out he thought I was going to grow my hair long, start wearing dresses and call myself Michaela. He imagined me mincing into his local pub and screaming my tits off. He's fine now, although we don't really discuss it.

I can never remember a time when I thought that women were attractive in a sexual sense. When I was six years old my mum gave me a page-boy haircut which I loved. One day this man came up to me in the street and said, 'Aren't you a lovely looking little girl?' I was so pleased and proud that he thought I was a girl.

Also, I had this recurring dream when I was seven. It involved me and my mum going on holiday with a strange man. We had two sleeping bags between us and every night my mum would call me into her sleeping bag. I didn't want to go. Then the strange man would ask if I wanted to get in with him. So I would climb in and it was all snug and cosy and I loved the feel of him.

So I always knew I was gay. My auntie Lil knew as well because when I was ten I used to go to her house, put a kilt on and pretend to be a Scottish dancer. My mother used to think that I was camp, but that maybe camp people could turn out straight. Not in my case though.

KIRSTY, BELFAST

My dad had guessed that me and my flatmate were more than good friends. I was going to tell my brother in my own good time. However, my dad decided that he should be told by someone in the family, before an outsider broke the news in a harsher way (even though I knew my dad's approach would hardly be gentle).

On the given night, when my dad returned from the pub – a rowdy local and obviously the only choice for intimate discussions – I asked if it had gone well, and what had been my brother's reaction.

'It's OK,' slurred my father, 'your brother was very manly

about the whole thing.'

Manly? What the hell does that mean for fuck's sake? Well, in this case it has meant the heterosexual man's usual lack of communication. We've never discussed it since.

RICHARD, LEICESTER

I decided to tell my friend, Pete. Coincidentally, his girlfriend was due back from the US that night. I came out with the classic line, 'Sit down, I've got something to tell you.'

He went terribly pale. Apparently, his immediate assumption was that his girlfriend had been killed in a plane crash. When he heard the details of my confession, he burst into hysterical laughter. He was just so relieved that the news was nothing more serious. It certainly made the situation less tense, he was great about it.

However, he told a lot of our other friends. This made me really angry at the time, I felt that somehow my thunder had been stolen.

DON, ILLINOIS

When I first came out to my friend, Fran, I didn't exactly say that I was gay. I just told her that I was in love with Peter. I was upset and emotional so Fran gave me a huge hug and said it was OK. Peter, unfortunately, turned out to be straight, and I never did tell him my feelings.

At the end of my sophomore year at college, when I was about eighteen, I was in love with a boy called Rob, who was also straight. I was very depressed at the time, and struggling with coming out. I tried to commit suicide by taking sleeping pills, and while I was in the hospital, my mum came down. I didn't tell her that I was gay, but I explained my feelings for Rob. She was really distressed to see me in that state, but she was also angry that I could let someone have such control over my life. She wasn't supportive really, she just yelled at me. Then she returned home, and I went back to classes as if nothing had happened.

I ended up having to drop out of school and go home, because I couldn't finish my semester. At home I talked to my dad. He held me and let me tell him how I felt. I don't remember him saying very much. So they both knew that I was in love with a boy, but I found out later that they didn't deduce from this that I was gay. After this incident, the subject was never raised again until after I had graduated, which was four years later. They had either blocked it out of their minds or forgotten about it.

One night at home, I called my mum into my room and said, 'Mum, you know I'm gay, right?' And she said, 'No.'

I was staggered. I asked her what she had imagined after the episode at college. She said she thought it was just a phase or something. So I felt like I had to come out to her for a second time. I also realized that I had to keep bringing the subject up to get it into their heads.

She didn't tell my dad about it, but about five months later, Fran accidentally did. She was at my parents' house while I was away at school. My dad took her aside and started asking her leading questions about me. She assumed that he was embarrassed, and was trying to bring the conversation round to my sexuality. So Fran said, 'You're talking about his being gay, aren't you?' He was stunned.

They had a long talk after that, but he never mentioned it to me until next time I was home. We were driving in the car and suddenly he said, 'Fran has told me something about you that I know isn't true, but I just wanted to check with you. She said you were gay.'

I told him that it was true and he immediately started to cry, saying that it was the worst thing that could ever happen to him. I said, 'That's a shame, seeing as it's the best thing that has ever happened to me.'

He still hasn't come to terms with it, we don't talk about it at all. My mum has come around a little bit and asks how my present relationship with Steve is going. They came to visit me in Chicago and Steve was with me. My father was polite and Steve spent the whole time with us. He talked a lot with my father and made a good impression, I think.

It's easier to be out when you're surrounded by other gay people. At the university there is a large gay community, and I have lots of friends. In Chicago I was living in **Boystown** so I had a supportive environment. It's harder at home, because I don't have any gay friends or community around me.

I feel that I came out to myself when I had the suicide attempt and that I was depressed for most of my adolescence. But when I came to terms with it and found a new identity for myself, I was very content. I began to feel secure and happy with my life, and that's the most important thing.

NOT OUT

Does your mother know that you're out?

ABBA

Sometimes the answer to the above question is an emphatic NO.

This section looks at different reasons behind the decision not to come out, at least not yet . . .

VICKY, WEST WALES

She wore very tight sports trousers and would shout at you for not getting in the shower. She was my gym teacher. I was eleven and I had a huge crush on her. One sad day she jumped too high on the trampoline, had an accident and had to leave the school. I was devastated at the time.

I can remember the exact moment that I knew I was a dyke. I was fourteen and looking at a picture of Kelly McGillis when I had a sudden revelation. I realized that I was gay and probably always would be. The picture had been on the wall for ages and I couldn't work out why I kept being drawn to it. Imagine, outed by Kelly McGillis.

After that there were the usual years of misery and self-loathing. I couldn't come out in a small Welsh village. There was a girl in the year below me who was brave enough to do it and they literally ran her out of town. She changed schools three times but kept getting beaten up. It was horrible. It's no better now.

Recently I went back home for a party and met an old friend. I was dead pleased to see her, so I kissed her cheek. Two people who used to be in my class immediately recoiled: 'What the fuck's wrong with you Vicky, are you a lezza or what?'

The first person I ever came out to was my friend Pilar. When I went to college I got involved with a dodgy woman. In fact she turned out to be the devil bitch from hell. I came home one day with a massive love-bite on my neck. My friend Pilar said, 'Where did you get that lovebite, Vicky?'

I got really defensive, 'Don't be silly, it's not a lovebite. I shut it in the door didn't I?' Though just how I thought I had shut the back of my neck in the door, I don't know. She seemed to accept this ridiculous explanation and didn't say any more about it.

But one night I couldn't bear it any longer and told her that I had something really bad to tell her, and that I didn't want her to be upset or stop being my friend.

I was being so melodramatic about it. It was almost a three-part mini-series, real *Martin Chuzzlewit* material. I told her that I was worried she'd be angry or disgusted. I think I built it up so much that when I finally told her it was a bit of an anti-climax. She thought I'd at least murdered someone.

She was fine about it, and from then on I told lots of people, everyone except my mum. Perhaps she knows, but I've never told her. I couldn't do it. She nearly found out courtesy of my landlady. One afternoon I feigned a headache, skived desk-top publishing and shimmied home to my bed and the demon woman.

We were happily ensconced when Mrs Cosby, my landlady, came in. She was appalled. She went mad, accusing me of bringing mice into the house and saying that I must be diseased.

Mrs Cosby took it upon herself to write to the university, telling them that I was a homosexual and not worth wasting college resources on. The head of the course called me into his office and told me that it was obviously a private matter between me and her and that it would have no bearing on the academic side of things. But it was very embarrassing. As for my parents, they also received a charming note from Mrs Cosby. It said that I was going to be dead within two years, that my unnatural sexual practices would kill me. It suggested that my father, as the head of the family, should endeavour to nip it in the bud before it was too late.

None of us wanted to discuss it. So we didn't. It was a conspiracy of silence. I felt vulnerable because my dad was funding my education and I really didn't want anything to threaten that. We have never mentioned it since.

There have been a few dodgy moments though. My mum phoned me once and asked me if I'd got something to tell her.

Me: No, not really mum.

Mum: Well when are you coming out, Vicky?

Me: Excuse me?

Mum: There's this book out from Llanelli Library called, *Coming Out: A History of Homosexuality*. Is that anything to do

Coming Out: A History of Homosexuality. Is that anything to do with you?

Me: Er . . . yes.

Mum: Well, why is it out on my ticket?

Me: Er . . . project.

Mum: Well it's three months overdue. I can't show my face up at that library now, they're going to think I'm a queer.

I posted it back.

I don't think I'll ever tell them now. We meet up infrequently, they look forward to it and we always have a wonderful time. How can I tell them that I have one of the most prominent jobs in the gay community and a very out lifestyle? They wouldn't understand, and the longer I leave it the harder it gets. What can I say to them?

'Oh, I came out five years ago, I've been lying to you for ages'? That's not going to make them feel like loving parents, which they are. Very much so. I do feel a bit shit about it because I could have come out, I just chose not to, and now it's almost impossible.

They would be upset about the times in the past when I've deceived them. Like the day they came for a surprise visit: I found myself telling my mum that my 'flatmate' slept alone in the big, cosy double bed and I was in the habit of curling up on two very small cushions in the living room. I tried to demonstrate how comfy they were. Ridiculous really.

My parents were really horrible and homophobic to my brother when they thought he was gay. He's not, but I think that's another reason why I haven't told my mum and probably never will.

HENRY, WARWICKSHIRE

The first bloke I slept with was Mark from work. He forgot his keys one night so I said he could stay with me. That was the beginning really. I was twenty-three.

My friend Sue was the first person I came out to. She had the hots for me in a big way. We used to sleep in the same bed and touch each other, but we never had sex. After I slept with Mark, I told Sue about it so that she would understand I was gay and stop fancying me so much. Mark already had an older boyfriend. When he heard about us, he offered to buy Mark a Jaguar sports car if he stopped seeing me. Mark went back, but he never got the Jaguar. He got a BMW convertible instead.

The following Christmas, Sue brought someone to a party who I started going out with. We've been together for over a year now. I feel about 90 per cent at ease with my sexuality, but I'm a bit embarrassed about being gay. I don't like people to know about it.

A few of my friends have heard that I'm gay, but I haven't told my parents. They are pretty homophobic although they do like Julian Clary. If they are watching the changing-room scenes after a rugby game and someone bends down in the showers, they always say things like, 'Whoa! Watch your back, lad.'

They paid for my education, so that stopped me from coming out because I didn't want them to reject me before I'd finished college.

While I was driving into work one day with my sister, she suddenly said, 'Henry, if I'm wrong just hit me, but are you gay?' I just said, 'Yes.' She hugged me and said she was glad I had told her the truth. She said that her friend had guessed anyway because I had nice hair.

After she left, I became worried that she would tell someone. I phoned her straight away from a call box to tell her not to, but she had already told my other sister. I called my other sister, only to find that she had already told her sister-in-law who had already told her friend. All I could say was, 'Well, don't tell mum.' If my mother knew, she would immediately tell her best friend, who would tell everyone else in the village.

Eventually I realize that I will have to tell my parents, because they will guess. I know a lot of people in the theatre and most of them are gay, so that will give me away really.

Two years ago, before I came out, I didn't know anyone who was gay. Last year I went to **Pride** for the first time. I was expecting it to be pretty awful and embarrassing and full of camp people like John Inman. I found being at the festival exciting and scary. I bumped into one friend which is what I was dreading, but she was OK about it. I enjoyed it a hundred times more than I expected to, and I will definitely go next year.

I think direct action is wonderful, but I wouldn't have the guts to do it myself. I went to a rally once in Trafalgar Square, for the Age of Consent campaign, but I was embarrassed because all the tourists were looking at us. I don't really like Edwina Currie even though I am a Tory.

Anyway, I don't think the age of consent should be sixteen. I think it should be eighteen for gays and straights.

JULIE, SOUTH WALES

I've never really sat down and said, 'Right I'm a lesbian now.' Basically, I just love having sex with women, and after the first time I thought, 'that was so fucking brilliant I must have more . . .'

I'm not out to my mother, we've never been close, and we don't have open communication channels between us. The benefits of telling her certainly don't outweigh the fear of rejection.

Sometimes I do feel the need to tell her, I think it would be sad if she died without knowing. But when I think it through, I decide there's no reason to tell her because I don't particularly want to get on better with her anyway. I definitely overcompensate for my mother not knowing by making sure other people are so aware of my sexuality. In fact I tell everyone except people in my family. I haven't even told my sister. But we haven't got a lot in common. My sister is a woman who painted her fingernails frosty pink during labour. At the first contraction she began to set her hair – all this so she'd look good on the video of the birth. So I don't really feel like we've got a huge amount of common ground.

I think that if I ever came out to my parents, my mother would scream the house down and my dad would say, 'Oh. Right. I see. OK,' without ever averting his eyes from the TV.

When I first realized how much I liked fucking women, I freaked out a bit and turned all religious. I went on a retreat and tried to put all the raunchy, dykey sex behind me. I was living in a hostel and I was involved with two Karens there. I was sleeping with one of them and I went on the retreat with the other. I thought that if I concentrated on God he would take away my lesbianism.

Returning from the retreat, I went to check my pigeon-hole for post. I had two letters. One from each Karen. The first, a booklet on God saying that Karen 1 hoped we could reach God together. The second, a scrawled note saying that Karen 2 hoped we could reach orgasm together. Soon. In fact why didn't I go up to her room right now? This minute.

This was my dilemma. My choice. My turning point . . .

Six months and many orgasms later, I took Karen home to meet my mother. My mother freaked out because she had never seen anyone who looked so dykey. Not a scrap of frosty pink nail varnish in sight.

When Karen went to the toilet my mother asked me if Karen was married. 'Mum,' I said. 'She's not the marrying kind.'

And we left it at that.

MICHELLE, SOUTHSEA

When I was thirteen years old, I told my best friend, Sally, that I thought I was bisexual and that I fancied her. For some time I had felt that perhaps men were not entirely what I wanted. There was something quite repulsive about all those dangly bits. She dismissed my feelings and even got quite cross with me. I also thought she was denying it because she felt threatened. I used to put my finger in the dimple on her chin. It really turned me on and I've had a weakness for dimples ever since. Part of me longed to try more, but I was afraid of losing her friendship.

After we left school and went our separate ways, we still kept in touch. Whenever we met, the air was charged between us, and several times after getting drunk we almost became physical. Somehow, it never quite happened.

When I was seventeen, I became very involved in the church, so I had to put aside my thoughts about my sexuality as it was incompatible with my religion. I got engaged and eventually told my fiancé about my feelings. He suggested that we have a threesome with Sally, so we decided to get her drunk and see if she would agree. She did. My memory of that night is of being fascinated by Sally's breasts, but ultimately feeling frustrated by the whole thing.

A few years later, she completely came out as a lesbian, and one night, after a few drinks, we had sex. I left afterwards feeling hugely excited, like a teenager after her first proper kiss. It was an important moment but I didn't really know what to do about it. I feel that my faith is in complete conflict with my sexuality, and it's a very hard struggle. I know that there are many gay Christians, but I don't know how they reconcile it in their minds.

My relationship with my fiancé ended and I seem to have come full circle. I am single at the moment and if I truly think about it I can't imagine ever being entirely happy with either sex. Each has desirable qualities which the other doesn't. I am more and more convinced that I was right at the age of thirteen to declare myself bisexual, and to resist labelling myself as either hetero- or homosexual for much of my life.

My mother thinks I'm a lesbian I'm sure, especially now she

knows that Sally is. She is just too scared to ask me. I could never tell her something like that to her face anyway. She'd be too upset. My brother's always been the rebel in our family, I have to be the good daughter.

Recently I have stopped going to church, because I feel that I can't live the lifestyle that I'm supposed to. I feel guilty, I suppose. I believe that the Bible condemns homosexuality, and that there isn't really a way to bring the two together.

MICHAEL, SURREY

I met my first real boyfriend while I was travelling around the world. I wanted to come out in England but felt unable to as I am an electrician and supposed to be butch and manly. Being abroad I was suddenly free. I could do as I liked and nobody back home would know.

While on a bus in Sydney I saw this beautiful Thai boy looking at me. I looked back of course, and we spent the whole journey glancing back and forth, as you do. I got off at my youth hostel and surprisingly enough, so did he. Being young and innocent, I didn't know what to do, but I was very bold. I went up to him and said, 'Would you like to go for a walk?' So we did, and ended up having a heavy petting session in the depths of a park in Sydney.

He lives with his family in Thailand, all of them in the same house. I go and stay there and his parents know that we sleep together. In Thailand, there are two sorts of gay men: the 'kratoyis' who are basically the transvestites plus anyone who is camp, and the straight-acting gay men. The first type are looked down upon, and the second type aren't talked about. So his family know we are a couple, they just don't mention it.

Because of this relationship, I felt that I should come out to my own family. So one Christmas, I took my brother aside and said to him, 'I thought I had better tell you that I'm gay.'

To my surprise, he said that he knew already and had been wondering when I was going to tell him. My father died two years ago and so I never had the chance to tell him. I always think, though, that he wouldn't have understood and so maybe it is better this way. Now I feel that everybody knows apart from my mother. I'm sure she must have some idea and I really want to tell her, it's just finding the right moment. It's the last thing I have to do before I'm fully 'out of the closet'.

RISHMA, EAST AFRICA

I most definitely am not out to my mother.

I am scared of her temper and the opinions of our extended family. It would be very stressful if I ever tried to come out, because it would not be accepted by my relatives. They are so involved in my life, you have no idea. They are consulted at every major juncture. When I was choosing 'A' levels, fifteen people sat me down and told me what subjects I was going to study.

As I get older and remain single, things will certainly become trickier. If I fall in love with a gorgeous woman and the relationship lasts, maybe I will feel more confident about raising the subject.

I have considered telling my family twice. On both of these occasions I have been in love. Glowing, rosy, happy and optimistic. However, the second relationship turned out so badly, that I lost all my confidence.

When I was fourteen, my mother sent my cousin in to ask if I was a lesbian. Mum was suspicious because me and my best friend were so inseparable at the time. I already knew I was a dyke, but I lied. I denied her accusation. I was madly in love with my best friend, but unfortunately she was straight. I was crazy about her for ten years. She wasn't interested until I finally began dating someone on the scene. Then I think she felt the loss and came on to me. Isn't life a strange spiral?

The subject hasn't been mentioned at home since I was fourteen. However, I once brought a girlfriend back and my mum was very rude to her. My mum has met lots of my friends, male and female, and she is always extremely polite and welcoming. Maybe she sensed that this woman was my lover, even though it was never said. My girlfriend stayed that night and mum spent hours pacing around on the creaky floor boards outside my room. Deep down I am almost certain that she knows I am gay, she just doesn't want to admit it.

When I had my nose pierced, my family screamed and generally went mad, especially as I had the stud on the right side which is considered bad luck in Hindu religion.

If my parents were more westernized, they might find it easier to accept me. We came to Britain about twenty years ago when I was seven. Recently I went back to Africa for two months. While I was there my mother was secretly calling my aunt and asking her to find a husband for me.

There are advantages to having a family like this. You feel secure knowing that they are always there to support you, even if they meddle at times. However there is pressure to justify your life, which can be hard, especially if you are gay.

A few months ago, I got a letter from two friends, saying that they had seen my picture on a lesbian video cover in Virgin Records. I was a bit worried, but my older relatives don't tend to go into record stores so I should be OK.

I can't imagine ever telling my mum that I'm a dyke. If I did I think she'd disown me for the first five or six years, perhaps send me away to another country and pray for change.

PHASED OUT

It's a phase, like the moon,
just a craze, there'll be a new phase soon,
she'll grow out of it, there's no doubt of it.

HARRIET POWELL,
SPARE TYRE THEATRE COMPANY

I'm sure that many people do go through phases. As a teenager I thought I was heterosexual but I soon grew out of it. However, the concept is often used to undermine the strength of real feelings . . .

STEVEN, IRELAND

The first time I would have described myself as being gay was at the age of fourteen. But I was having sex with men long before that, and even prior to puberty I used to fantasize about my classmates. It was an all-boys grammar school and we played a lot of contact sports. Many straight adolescents play these games anyway so it was easy to join in. It was all very up front and there was no suggestion of anything other than boys being boys. We used to grab each other's balls and laugh, that kind of thing.

It slowly dawned on me that I was getting quite passionate about one or two men in particular. I hated rugby anyway, but as soon as possible I chose the swimming option. We got to do life-saving which basically meant hugging men while towing them up and down the pool. Then we got changed together afterwards.

It was great, a lot of fun, but at this stage never explicitly sexual. We were all becoming too self-conscious about our bodies and our sexualities for it to go any further. However, I realized that some of these guys made me feel really horny and I

59

accepted it, but only on the terms that it was a phase I was going through.

This was the received wisdom at fourteen. I heard adults talking of 'passing phases' so I didn't get stressed out about my feelings at all. I just presumed it was something I was going through that I would grow out of.

However, by sixteen, I felt enormously perturbed. I became aware that the passions weren't fading, but in fact getting stronger. The fantasies were becoming more dominant, and I began to doubt the pervasive concept of 'the phase' and feel frightened.

The growing horror of realizing that I might be a faggot quite appalled me, to the extent that I began a programme of self-oppression, brain-washing myself into suppressing my feelings.

I would count the number of times that I masturbated in a week, and meticulously monitor what my fantasies were about. I would actively try to think about women when I wanked, and reward myself hugely if it was successful.

If I fantasized about men I would punish myself severely, mentally beat myself up, saying inside my head, 'You dirty, horrible person.' I was still clinging on to an idea that when I met the right woman, and I actually had some physical contact with her, a new and brighter sexuality would be revealed to me.

For two very powerful years, between sixteen and eighteen, I was so tough on myself. It was really heavy shit, and still the 'correct' sexuality eluded me.

Leaving home, I turned to drugs and lost about a year in a chemically induced stupor of despair. I remember one particularly tripped-out, spacey afternoon, I was lying on someone's living-room floor, and I began to realize that I probably was queer. I didn't like the idea, but I was going to have to face up to it somehow.

It took a lot of strength, but I just had to accept that however hard I ran, I couldn't get away from the feelings and nastiness inside me. They had to come out, and so did I.

CAROLYN, BIRMINGHAM

We have never found it easy to talk about things in my family. I was twenty-five the first time I mentioned my 'feelings' to my parents. Well, I say my parents but it was really just my mum. Mums always seem to be the listeners, don't they?

I was terribly upset because my first major relationship had just broken up. My mum wasn't happy when she realized that I was crying over a woman. She tried to reassure me: 'Don't worry dear. One of these days you'll meet someone really nice, someone like your father.'

Since then I've tried unsuccessfully to discuss it with her. I do feel that being unable to communicate about such a vital part of my life cuts me off from my mum. But when I mention it, I can see her tensing up. Sometimes she says that she doesn't mind as long as I'm happy. But I think that if I actually met someone important, I wouldn't feel confident about taking her home.

They are parents who find it difficult to accept this type of thing. So I try to respect the problems they have and not throw it at them. They have a lot to cope with in their lives besides me and I genuinely don't want to burden them. It's sad that we can't talk about it though. They would never think of saying, 'How are you? Have you met anyone special?'

I'm forty-three now, and I know that my mother presumes I'm going through a phase: a never-ending phase.

I think I've always known that I was gay, but I've never been very sexually active. Some people seem to have relationship after relationship, but I've never felt interested in that. I've always been attracted to my own sex though. Always.

I remember when I was about nineteen or twenty, realizing that I really wanted to go out with a woman. I had lots of friendships and I used to hope that these would become more, but they never did. I just had to come to terms with the way that these women made me feel.

The first relationship I actually had was when I was twenty-five. It was with a married woman who had three children. It was an amazing experience. One day our eyes just met in the street. She was getting out of her car and I was walking past her drive-way. That simple. It was absolute magic. I'd never felt anything like it, and unfortunately I never have since.

When it ended, the pain was unbelievable. I know other people must have been through break-ups like this, but I didn't know that it was possible to hurt so much. I had to take a week off work. I thought I was going to have a nervous breakdown. I went home to talk to my mum, but as you know, that wasn't very successful.

Consequently, I switched myself off. I've never really let go in a relationship since. I was so hurt, my mind told me, 'You can't afford to be like this ever again.' It was harder to handle than a death.

I have three younger brothers and sisters. The youngest one knows and is very happy about it, which is great. The other two don't know because I have very little to do with them. I also feel that neither of them is stable enough to deal with it. I think they would cause my parents a lot of hassle. They would go back and whinge and whine to mum and it would just be too sad for her.

On another level, it's none of their business, because they're not interested in me anyway. My friends know, and that's the main thing. I needed to tell them and be accepted. This shouldn't be so important to me, but it is.

As for my dad, he's a very staunch Catholic. To him, it is unheard of, it's not real. He wouldn't even discuss it. If I ever mentioned it, he'd refer me to the church's line. I still go to church. I don't have a problem with that or feel that Christ would discriminate in his love.

I am out as far as possible at work. I teach in an all-girls school. I am a professional and I have a responsibility to young minds. It's not my job to lead them in any direction or thought other than in the subject I teach.

Obviously, sexuality comes up in lessons sometimes; I need to feel that I can be neutral in the statements I make. For example, if a child says that they don't like the idea of a certain character on TV being gay, I try to ask them why, instead of condemning their views. I don't feel the need to fight for the cause, but I like to make young people think through their opinions. Often, it's fellow pupils who will put forward the opposite side of the argument.

I'm out to my friends on the staff. I didn't want to hide because you always run the risk of a blackmail element creeping in. I don't want that.

I'd love to take the right person to the staff Christmas meal, and to have the chance to be proud of someone.

FI, LEICESTER

My best mate, who was straight, was the first person I actively came out to. She prompted it by saying, 'I know what's going on, you know.'

She told me that my mother had been reading my post, and had discovered my secret. At the time I wasn't too annoyed, I was just relieved that I didn't have to start from scratch in coming out to her. Now when I think back, I get more angry about the invasion of my privacy.

My mother's reaction was pretty clichéd really. She thought that it was a phase, and that all I needed was a nice boyfriend.

The following Christmas, I met all my old school friends in the pub for a drink. I had decided that this was my moment. I was planning to come out to all of them, which I did. One woman physically flinched as I said it, and subtly moved away from me.

That made me feel a bit strange and vulnerable. Everyone else there was fine about it. She left as soon as possible.

Six years later, my mum left my dad. She has told me since that she feels her own sexuality could have gone either way at that point. She had previously explained my lesbianism to herself by saying that it was due to bad experiences as a child and being scared of men. After she split up from my dad she saw things differently. She realized that she had missed out on intimacy, and saw me enjoying it with other women. Mum realized at that point that being gay was not a phase.

I felt hugely relieved and empowered by her change of feeling. Coming out made me a stronger and more confident person. If my mother accepts me, there is no one I need to apologize to for what I am.

MICHAEL, GUILDFORD

When I first came out to my friend Simone at the age of twelve, I told her that I thought I was bisexual. It was really trendy to be 'bi' then, as opposed to gay. We were walking down my street at the time, aptly called Mincing Lane.

I told Simone that I fancied her boyfriend. I think he knew I had a big crush on him because I talked about gay things a lot. She was very supportive about it all anyway, and I felt great relief after telling her. The trouble was, we never managed to raise the subject again, and I carried on going out with girls. Pretty soon after, Simone and her boyfriend split up, and he started dating my girlfriend. I was very upset, but not, as everyone supposed, because I wanted her back. I wanted him.

I had no close friends at school when I was young. I was fairly popular, but everyone kept their distance. I was a loner most of the time and started bunking off school. Eventually, the teacher told my parents and they challenged me one night, asking what was wrong. I told them that I thought I was bisexual. 'Gay' somehow seemed much too appalling. I wanted to blame them for it, I felt that it was their fault that I was gay.

I was very isolated at school. No one in my class was as camp. In fact, no one was like me at all; I felt different. When we played sports, we had separate teams for girls and boys. The boys were all obsessed with winning, and the girls all chatted, giggled and had fun. I was desperate to be in the girls' team.

I told my parents all this and they were kind about it. They said that it was a phase, my dad even said that he had gone through something similar. I knew inside that it was permanent though. I was embarrassed and almost disgusted by it.

I had a friend next door called Gavin Quick. We used to do dares and play truth games. Things started to develop beyond that, and one day he asked if he could wank me off. I was so ignorant that I didn't know what he meant. I just said, 'Yes, OK.'

So he did the necessaries, and I was amazed because I didn't know what was coming. Literally. That was my first sexual experience. I was fourteen then, and after that I knew for sure what I was.

For the next two years I was very depressed. I knew what I wanted, but I didn't know what to do, or who to talk to about it. I remember my biology teacher telling me not to be camp. I had to look it up in the dictionary, and when I did I was shocked. I had thought I was putting on a good act.

When I was sixteen I got a job in Woolworths and met a man who worked in Boots. He was the first out gay person I had ever encountered. His boyfriend, Neil, was the most amazing man. He was witty, outrageous, and told the world that he was gay. Everyone seemed to love him. He was my first role model. I thought, 'This is who I want to be.'

So I started going around with him, and being influenced by him. Neil and I both worked behind a bar and were very camp. I used to wear make-up and blue eyeliner because I thought that was the 'in' thing to do. I had spiky, red hair, and diamante jewellery that would put Liz Taylor to shame. We wore boiler-suit tops and looked like extras from Village People. We bought our clothes from Chelsea Girl. For the first time, I realized that even if you weren't normal you could still have fun and be outrageous.

We were wild and camp for a while, but suddenly I saw through it all. I realized that Neil was lonely and sad, and he was putting on a huge front. I didn't want to be the same, so I started going to the local gay pub. The people there wore jeans and trainers and were ordinary. I even saw my first lesbians. Basically, they were normal people with normal lives and I realized that these were good role models for me. I met my first boyfriend at that pub.

While we were going out, my mum read my diary and discovered that every night I had a date with Mark. She marched into the living room and asked me who he was. I was watching *Dynasty* at the time, and the sight of **Steven Carrington** gave me courage. I was proud of my relationship and I didn't see being gay as an abnormal lifestyle anymore. So, taking a deep breath I said, 'He's my boyfriend actually.'

My mum went up the wall. She smashed the mug she was holding and started shouting insults at me. I felt anger towards her for the first time. She said she would phone my boyfriend and tell him he could never see me again. With that, she stormed out of the room. I was stunned, so I went up to my room.

A few minutes later she came up. She hadn't phoned Mark. I was crying and so was she. She told me that she was terribly worried about AIDS. This was March 1986 and my mother believed everything she read in the papers. We talked for a while and as she walked out the door she said, 'Your dad's going to kill you, you know.'

I was terrified. I could hear her in the kitchen, telling him. Then he came up to my bedroom. I grabbed a copy of *Shoot* football magazine, my dad's favourite, and pretended to be reading it when he walked in.

All he said was that he knew I'd been miserable, and he'd noticed the change since I started seeing Mark. He said it was no big deal being gay and that happiness was the important thing. My dad was perfect. He even hugged me.

I KNOW YOU'RE OUT THERE

No I didn't dig deep,
I did not want to know,
well you don't interfere
when you're scared of the things
you might hear.

MARTI WEBB

Many parents actually know deep down that their child is gay. Some suspect it from recent behaviour, and others say that they have known for years, since early childhood in certain cases . . .

KATHERINE, LONDON

The first person I came out to was the woman who made me realize that I was a lesbian. She was a teacher at the college in Brighton where I was training, and she used to give me a lift to work. I knew she was a feminist, and as far as I was concerned then, all feminists were lesbians.

Although I had been falling in love with women for a couple of years, well, all my life really, I still didn't think that I was a lesbian. The thing is, I didn't know what it meant, I had never heard the word said out loud. I remember my mother referring to an old family friend as a 'spooky dyke' and wondering what that was all about. Basically, I had all the lesbian ingredients there, but no recipe yet.

One morning, in the car my teacher friend began telling me about a women-only disco she had been to. She asked me if I would be interested in going. I thought, 'How wonderful. Imagine being able to dance without waiting for a man to ask you.' I immediately said yes.

Then she started telling me about her new 'lodger', a female nurse, and added, 'You understand, of course, that no one at college knows my leanings.' At that moment it was as if a huge hammer had fallen out of the sky on to my head, and I thought, 'Oh my God! That's it. That's what I am.'

Over the next few days, I was in turmoil with the thought of being a lesbian. I decided that I had to tell this woman, because saying it out loud would confirm my sexuality in my own mind.

So the next morning I got into her 2CV with my head full of what I was going to say. But somehow, whenever I tried to begin, I just couldn't think of the right words. I spent the entire journey wrestling with myself until I saw the school gates looming up ahead of us. I realized that now had to be my moment so I summoned up my courage and started gabbling, 'You know what you were talking about the other day? Well, I think I'm one too.'

She was very supportive and whisked me off on a tour of the Brighton lesbian scene. It completely blew my mind. I decided that if you weren't a dyke when you arrived in Brighton, you were certainly one when you left.

Two months later, I knew that I had to tell my mum. I didn't want to start lying to her about my life, as this would make our relationship meaningless.

So, on the chosen weekend, I went home to see her. I felt like a different person. I had a new social life, a new sexuality and even my menstrual cycle had changed! I had spent all my life being the good elder daughter and now I was liberated.

My mother was asleep when I arrived, so I sat and read my book, **Boy's Own Story** by Edmund White. When she awoke, she asked me what I was reading. I told her and she started interrogating me as she knew what the book was about. I began to blush, so she really pushed the questions. I stuttered and stammered for a while and then said, very quickly, 'I think I might be.'

At that moment, my mother fainted and fell on to the floor in front of me, sending her tea tray flying into the air. She was out cold.

She came round fairly quickly, and as I knelt by her side she looked directly at me and said, 'You know Katherine, I was only saying yesterday that nobody seems to faint any more.'

She was calm. I, on the other hand, was sobbing loudly as I mopped cold tea off the sofa. We spent the rest of the afternoon talking and she asked me lots of questions. She kept insisting that I could still get married, citing Vita Sackville-West and Harold Nicolson: 'Didn't they have a fruitful marriage and do some wonderful gardening?' She also told me that everyone finds relationships with men difficult and 'you just have to keep trying'. She even suggested that I shouldn't have sex, which I thought was a bit unfair. I was having to justify myself and I didn't feel ready to do that.

Nowadays she is fine about it and has even met my girlfriend. She was relieved that my partner wasn't over six foot with very short hair. She should have seen the last one. She is slightly disturbed by the fact that my partner is only five years younger than she is, but we manage.

Shortly after I told my mum, I received a very sweet letter from my stepfather, saying that he knew and it made no difference to him. He also mentioned that he had had passionate affairs with boys at school, which had turned out to be a passing phase. My real father, however, was a different story.

My mother had begged me not to tell him, saying that as I was his only daughter, it would break his heart. I colluded with this for years but eventually decided that I couldn't keep up the pretence any longer. I asked him to meet me for dinner, saying I had something important to tell him.

During the evening, my courage deserted me, and as had been the case years earlier, I didn't know how to begin. My father tried prompting me into telling him my big secret, but I went through the entire meal evading questions. When we got to the coffee stage he was getting desperate, and the conversation went something like:

Dad: Come on then, what's the big secret?

Me: I'm going out with a woman.

Dad: Yes, I know.

Me: Sorry, what?

Dad: Your mother told me six months ago.

That was the first great fight I had with my mother. I wasn't angry that she had told him, it was just that if she had mentioned it to me, I would have been spared the trauma of coming out to him. I was so shocked at this turn of events, that it was only when I got home that night that I realized I hadn't asked my dad what he thought about my being a lesbian.

Since then, my father has been very accepting. He has no problem introducing me and my girlfriend as a couple to friends and colleagues. This surprised me as he pays no lip service to equal opportunities, but in practice he comes up with the goods.

Looking back at my childhood, my mother has told me that she strongly suspected my sexuality from quite a young age. She had very socialized ideas about how a lesbian looks and acts, and says that she watched me, as a child, growing into this stereotype in front of her eyes. She said that the moment I told her, she felt a wave of knowledge coming up from her womb which literally knocked her out. She says that she looked at her young child and thought, 'My daughter is a lesbian.'

She says that she has always known.

JOSÉ, GRAN CANARIA

I was sixteen, and in a coffee bar with my fourteen-year-old sister. I knew deep down inside myself that I was gay, but I certainly hadn't discussed it with my sister.

A well-known tarot card reader was coming round the café, offering her services to people. I knew that she was talented and perceptive. Friends had told me of uncannily accurate information that she had provided them with.

When she reached our table, I indicated that I would like to have a reading, but later when my sister had gone home. All ears, my little sister piped up, 'You just don't want me to be here when the cards show that you're a homosexual.'

NIGEL, ROTHERHAM

My mother says that she has always known. Apparently there is corroborative evidence from my early years: tales that have become family mythology.

We were on holiday once in Bridlington. My nana gave me and my brother a pound each to spend on the pier. This was a long time ago because I was only about five, and my brother was seven. It seemed like a huge amount of money and we were both very excited.

I remember scouring the shops and stalls looking for a bargain. This was probably the start of my shopping addiction, so I should sue my grandmother and send her my credit card bills.

Anyway, the story goes that half an hour later my brother catapulted into view brandishing a machine gun with 'realistic sound effects'. I followed behind, skipping down the pier, wearing a long ginger wig with plaits. My granny screamed and slapped me, and a tussle ensued over the wig. I think I won.

The following Christmas, all the cousins were put in a room to play with newspaper. This was Rotherham entertainment at its best. My uncle was showing us how to make palm trees, and all the kids were copying him. I thought that was terribly tedious, and instead, fashioned a rather swish grass skirt and sashayed into the living room. Most of my relatives were too drunk to pay attention. My nana fainted, but no one really noticed as she did that all the time anyway.

OUT OF THE MOUTHS . . .

The world is dark and wild.
Stay a child while you can be a child.
STEPHEN SONDHEIM

As the following stories illustrate, children are very accepting of difference.

However, as we are aware, socialization results in the young hearing that homosexuality is 'abnormal', and therefore wrong. Small wonder that many gay people torture themselves with years of self-loathing during the coming out process.

Ever the optimist, I hope that perhaps, as we cruise towards the twenty-first century and our family structures become even more diverse, a wider cross-section of young people will be able to carry their open minds through into adulthood. Let us dream of the day when homophobic desk graffiti, scratched into the varnish with a bent compass, is a thing of the past.

CLAIR, MINNEAPOLIS

One day I overheard a conversation between my four-year-old son, Mac, and his best friend. The friend asked Mac where his daddy was. Mac said that he didn't have one.

'Why?' asked the friend.

'Because I've got two mummies, silly,' replied Mac patiently, as if it was the most obvious thing in the world.

There was a short silence, then the friend said, 'You're such a lucky duck Mac, you've got two mummies.'

ISLA, LONDON

My children know and accept me for what I am. My little boy, who is six, wants to be a lesbian when he grows up.

NIGEL, ROTHERHAM

My sister has got two children, who are eight and nine. A few months ago she was driving along, and the kids were fighting in the back, calling each other 'a gay' as an insult. She turned to them and said, 'Be quiet you two, you don't even know what a gay is.'

They both protested that they did, saying that it was a boy who liked another boy. My sister snapped back at them, 'Yes, well your Uncle Nigel's one of those.' They both went very quiet.

Last Christmas when I saw them, they were fascinated with me, saying, 'Uncle Nigel, have you got a girlfriend?'

I replied, 'You know that I've got a boyfriend.'

'Is Ray your boyfriend, Uncle Nigel?' they asked. I gritted my teeth, 'Not any more, children. Ray and I aren't friends any more.'

That was the best way I could think of to tell them that the bastard had dumped me.

STEVE, GEORGIA

I'm pretty sure that my niece and nephew are clued into the situation. Last Christmas their present to me was a small statue of Glenda the Good Witch, from the *Wizard of Oz*. So I guess they know that their Uncle Steve is a friend of Dorothy.

Before my mother died, she told me that she had always intended to have a daughter. Apparently, when I was born, she had cried for a week because she wanted a girl. It's a pity she didn't live long enough to see that she got one.

EMILY, WOLVERHAMPTOM

When my friend came round for coffee, her six-year-old daughter used to play in the bedroom. One day when I went in to fetch her, she said, 'Do you and Rosa both sleep in the same bed?'

I gulped, feeling as though I had been caught doing something naughty. 'Yes,' I replied, trying to sound casual.

She looked at me with large, innocent eyes. 'Why?' she asked.

'Well . . .' I began unsteadily, 'Your mum sleeps with her boyfriend, doesn't she? So me and Rosa sleep together. It's the same thing.'

She wasn't going to let me off that easily, 'But you're two girls, why do two girls sleep together?'

I was completely stuck now and had to give in. I rushed back to my friend in a panic and told her that her child was asking about lesbians and what should I say? My friend was completely relaxed about it.

'Just tell her that you love each other,' she said.

I hadn't thought of that.

TAKING OUT THE STING

Gay sera, sera,
whatever will be, will be,
it's your sexuality,
Gay sera, sera.

A QUEER ANTHEM
BORROWED FROM DORIS DAY

Occasionally people don't feel able to come out completely, so they try to water down the news and avoid hurting their family. Parents can also be adept at this. Some may find the concept of their own child's homosexuality impossible to accept, so they bend the truth to convince themselves that it's not as bad as they think . . .

SUSAN, WINKLEIGH

My initial coming out statement, made to my friend Erin, was really rather tentative: 'I think I might be bisexual, but I'm not sure, I mean the idea doesn't totally repulse me.'

We were having one of those deep confessional sessions after four pints of lager where you both tell a Big Secret. I went first. Her secret was that she fancied me. So I kissed her. The next day she went to America for a year. During her stay with me, we had been sleeping in the same bed with no clothes on, but for some reason I had not thought this was unusual. It was a single bed, the weather was warm, and ventilation is important.

But when she told me she fancied me, I was really surprised. I was shocked that Erin, very straight girlie with incredibly long blonde hair, was a dyke.

Soon after that, I moved from the liberal college where I had come out, to Devon. Of course I went straight back in, and closed the door, as you do in Devon. However, I did fall madly in love with a girl there, and after a year of build-up we managed to have a relationship. It was an exhausting courtship.

My mother knows I'm a lesbian because my sister told her, sort of like a proxy vote. My sister found out when I split up with the girlfriend I was living with. I was moving out and my sister wanted to know why.

She was sitting at the kitchen table eating a huge saveloy when I came into the room. 'So why can't you carry on living with Sarah?' she asked.

'Well, because we're not together any more,' I answered in a very matter-of-fact voice.

'What do you mean?' she replied, waving the sausage at me. 'Aren't you friends any more?'

'No' I said calmly, 'We're not going out any more.'

At this point, my sister put the humongous sausage in her mouth and took a bite; a rather over-exaggerated, dramatic sort of a bite. I stood looking at her and her sausage and thought how symbolic life seemed to be sometimes.

So my sister, being a bit of a bitch, told my mother. But not immediately.

I was in a show, playing a lesbian character. My mother knew this and used to laugh about it saying, 'You're not trying to tell us something are you, Susan?'

I used to laugh back and say, 'No, no . . . no.'

She was obviously thinking about it, because one day she said to me, 'The thing I don't understand about lesbians is how do they find each other?'

She was clearly suspicious about me, so of course she asked my sister who immediately told her. When I heard about this, I wrote my mother a letter saying things like, 'I'm just the same person I was yesterday . . .' and so on.

My mother countered this with radio silence for about a fortnight, then asked to see me. Her first comment was, 'Well,

Susan, I just think you're a bit **AC/DC**.'

Eight years on, this still sums up her view of my sexuality. I stopped going out with boys ten years ago, and in that time I have had long-term significant relationships with women that my mother has met. And yet still, she doesn't take it fully on board. When I think about it, I always tell myself that I must have a serious talk with my parents . . . tomorrow.

I'd like to come out to more relatives, but not eighty-four-year-old grandmothers, because it's a bit awkward. So Nana can't come round for tea.

TRENT, THE MIDLANDS

We went up to the rugby club for a walk. It's where we always went when I was little, so the place was full of memories for me; even more so now. Perhaps in future years there will be a blue plaque on the side of a tree saying, 'Trent came out here – April 1987.' In my mind the event has that magnitude.

My dad said that it didn't surprise him, but then added, 'Please tell me there is some hope you won't always be like this.'

We were both crying. I didn't really know what to say so I just stated the simple truth of the situation, 'Dad, I've met someone, and I know I'll never feel for a woman what I feel for this guy.'

Since then, my parents have been very supportive, and I do believe that ultimately they just want me to be happy.

But looking back, I think I owe thanks to the man who built my mum and dad's extension. He was a friend of theirs, and he ran off with another builder when he was forty-five, leaving his wife and children behind. They liked him very much, but they didn't like the deception involved. I think they were relieved that I hadn't got involved in something complicated and hurtful. They would never have wanted me to live a lie.

Recently my boyfriend and I built a wall for my parents, and I think it somehow reassured them – because it proved we weren't too effeminate, but in fact really butch! A bit like the man who built their extension . . .

TODD, CHICAGO

My friend Naverro was the first person I told that I was gay. We met at college and had a bit of a romance. When I knew that I was ready to come out, I told her first because I trusted her most. And apart from the fact that she kept on saying, 'Are you *sure* that you're not bisexual?' she was great.

I told my mum and dad about six months later. We were in the lounge of my student co-operative, sitting on a wheatgerm sofa. My dad was very concerned and serious. He wanted to know how I was going to cope with it, and if it would affect my career. Mum was upset and quiet at first. I didn't know at the time that they were having major marital problems, so I probably picked the worst moment to come out. She told me later that she had felt unable to function at that time. After the initial shock, they got much better about it. Nowadays, they totally accept my sexuality. I'm very lucky really.

NIGEL, ROTHERHAM

In my teens I thought that I should confirm my mother's suspicions and make the whole thing official. When I told her she said, 'What you mean is that you're bisexual, Nigel.'

'No mum, we're talking about the whole hog here. Fully gay.'

'But Nigel, you were always so fond of Helen Anderson. I had high hopes for her.'

'Mum, I was nine.'

After I'd told my mum, I felt incredibly free. I'd known that I was definitely gay by the age of eleven, but it had taken me seven years to vocalize it. When I was fourteen, I thought that I would burst unless I said it out loud, so I used to repeat it when I was alone, and walking down the street: 'I'm gay, I'm gay, I'm gay . . .' It was like some sort of mantra.

That year, I had half the kids on the school register: Robert, Ricky, Colin and George. Everyone, in fact, except Peter. He said that he was straight, and at fourteen he should know, so I respected that.

I asked my mum to tell dad while I was out. Afterwards he went for a long drive. When he got back he seemed fine. Dad never mentioned it directly but used to say things like, 'Have you made any new "friends" lately?'

I wish he'd seen me happy before he died.

I took my brother, Jonathan, to a gay bar to try and tell him. But he told me really:

Jonathan: You like it here, don't you Nigel?

Me: Yeah.

Jonathan: You feel really at ease here, don't you Nigel?

Me: Yeah.

Jonathan: You're gay, aren't you Nigel?

Me: Yeah.

Jonathan: I think sex is fantastic. I love it, and I want you to love it too. I don't care whether it is with a man or a woman, as long as you enjoy it.

I have been trying to follow his example over the years.

HELP OUT

**Help me if you can, I'm feeling down,
And I do appreciate you being round.**

THE BEATLES

Sometimes the hinges on the closet door seem a bit stiff, and it takes a friend to help us open up and realize that things can be much brighter on the outside.

Others in this section managed to squeeze out themselves, without even snagging their best jersey on a coat hanger. However, help and support were still necessary, and available. Communication seems to be the key – to more than just the closet.

ROSIE, GLASGOW

The first person I told was my gay friend, Neil. I met him while we were doing nursing training. He was a very positive role model; a popular person who seemed to be at ease with his sexuality and to be really enjoying his life. I hadn't really admitted to myself that I was a lesbian. This was despite the fact that I'd had sex with my best friend at school.

After this I kept thinking that I wanted to have sex with more women, but I decided that I couldn't actually be a lesbian, because all the dykes I knew were quite butch, and I didn't find them particularly attractive. Ironically, my first girlfriend was pretty butch and used to crush beer cans in one hand. But that's another story.

Soon after I met Neil, we went out and got very drunk. I sat staring at a group of lesbians having a wonderful time together and when I felt drunk enough, the conversation went something like this:

Me: What would you say if I said I was a lesbian?

Neil: I'd say that I've always wondered.

Me: Why?

Neil: Well, for one, you're certainly not interested in straight men at all.

Me: Oh.

Neil: Look, I'll send my dyke friend Paula round to have a chat with you in the morning, OK?

Me: OK.

Neil: Good. Right then, that's settled. Are you going to the bar to get the drinks then?

Me: Yes.

I was a woman of few words at that time. Also, I was amazed that I'd just come out to two people; myself, and my best friend.

Well, sure enough, Paula came round the next morning, bearing croissants and orange juice. We did have a chat, but we also had wild, abandoned, raunchy lesbian sex, barely having time to remove our nurses' uniforms.

Since then, there's been no looking back.

COLIN, IRELAND

The first person I came out to was my girlfriend, Alison. She was very perturbed.

Looking back on the situation I was quite mean to her. I was nineteen and I think I'd already decided I was gay. However, she set her hat at me, and was determined to make us an item. This determination gave me the opportunity to 'test' myself. I still had a last lingering thought that I might be straight and I just hadn't met the right girl yet. In fact I hadn't met any girls.

So Alison was the first one really, and certainly the only girl I'd slept with. The others had been very much 'kiss-on-the-cheek' type relationships. I effectively used Alison as an experiment, and the few months that I was with her really clarified my own sexuality.

She was a wonderful woman, very strong. So finally one night in bed I told her I was gay. She was absolutely brilliant. And despite the fact that she wasn't terribly happy about it, still managed to be incredibly supportive.

It got more difficult over the next few weeks, because she was still very keen on me. I was on this voyage of discovery and she wanted to know where this left her. Eventually I was forced to admit that, despite being very fond of her, there was something missing that only a man could provide.

Ultimately this was very cruel, and a horrible emotional experience for Alison. It made her feel redundant and useless. I was her friend. I respected her, but I was demolishing her sexuality, and I regret that this fantastic woman had to go through such a damaging process.

That's why I get furious with men who know they're queer and still marry straight women. I think they're despicable.

DAVID, LEICESTER

I am thirty now, and I have only thought of myself as gay for the last couple of years. Before that I was in a straight relationship for quite some time. Three months ago I went to see my parents and came out to them. They were absolutely fine about it. They told me to be careful of HIV and AIDS and said they hoped that I was happy.

The first person I came out to was my ex-girlfriend who was very supportive. A couple of my brothers-in-law have been a little bit negative, saying that it's unnatural and shouldn't be allowed, but I don't think they're that bothered, because I'm not their brother.

I think that for most of my life I could have gone either way. It just so happens that I got into a straight relationship first. The last few years though, I have looked at women less and less, and now I don't at all.

I was very nervous before telling my parents because I had heard so many stories about friends getting bad reactions, so I was relieved that they took it so well.

A few weeks ago I started coming out at work, and most people have been OK about it.

I think that as time goes on and lots of people come out, things will get easier because more and more people will know someone who is gay.

STEVE, GEORGIA

With hindsight, I should have figured out that I was gay at about eight or nine. Instead, it all happened at college.

Each summer I went to Washington, to work at Capitol Hill. One particular summer, I decided to join a gym there. So I went around the city checking out all the places, and having a look around. That evening, I was sitting on the bed removing my sneakers when it suddenly struck me. The gym I liked best was the one where I could cruise the most men! I couldn't believe it. I had never considered such a thing before. Within about twenty minutes I had come to the conclusion that I was gay. I was so happy, I joined the gym immediately.

West Virginia is a pretty backward state. There are plenty of bible-thumpers there, and I realized at an early age that there was a better life beyond it. Shortly after my seventeenth birthday, I went to Washington DC to finish high school. The day I got on that plane was one of the happiest of my life.

I started dating girls at the age of sixteen. Looking back, I was probably out as a gay man for two years before I'd had sex with as many men as women. I dated a girl at college for about six months. I started to think that I could be happy on both sides of the fence. I was also seeing a guy who gave me the nickname 'Huggy Bear'. Other people began using this name, and one day, my girlfriend asked me how I got it. I told her that someone I was seeing called me that.

I explained he was a guy, called Danny, expecting her to freak out, but she just said, 'I'm not surprised.' Then she added, very calmly, 'If you want to sleep with men, it's fine, so long as I still get attention.' I wish she had slapped me or insulted me. But she was too much of a lady.

The first person that I voluntarily came out to was my boss at the Capitol Building, Anne. One morning I just decided that I was going to tell her. I talked for about two or three hours, explaining the sudden revelation that I'd had while choosing a gym. I described how I felt about myself and hoped that she would understand. Suddenly, she turned to me and said, 'You have no idea that I'm a lesbian, do you?'

I was stunned. Anne immediately took me to the best lesbian bar in Washington for a celebratory drink.

I am lucky in that I have no family to answer to about my sexuality, which seems to be why so many people are stuck in the closet. My mother died when I was fourteen, and soon after my father's remarriage, we were all kicked out of the house.

Once I realized that sleeping with men was what I wanted to do, I went through a stage of bedding every man I could get my hands on. I went wild. If I'd had parents to worry about, I would have been much more careful about my activities.

I am out to my eldest brother and his wife, Candy, who are the closest people to me in my remaining family. While at college, I dated an orthopaedic surgeon from Boston, who paid for me to fly over and see him every weekend. As I was a poor student, Candy guessed that something was going on. When I eventually confessed, she said that she had known for a year, but was glad I had told her. We had always been very close and she didn't want any secrets to come between us.

My brother is a rather boring accountant, and I wasn't sure how he would take the news. When Candy told him, he apparently said, 'I'm worried about Steve getting through college, I'm worried about his grades, but I really don't give a shit who he sleeps with.'

SARIT, ISRAEL

My mother was the last person I came out to. I came to England a year ago and my brother came over to visit me. When he asked me about boyfriends, I told him that I was a lesbian. He was shocked at first, asked for a day to get used to the idea, and then decided that I was still his sister.

After that, I was desperate to tell my mum. I just couldn't wait so I went to Israel to tell her. I thought that she might already know, because all the signs were there when I was a kid: I was a real tomboy and I never had any boyfriends or crushes on boys.

When I arrived, she was very pleased to see me. I was incredibly anxious about telling her. I wanted to do it as soon as possible. While the family were sitting around talking, she asked me if I had a boyfriend, so I just said, 'I'm gay.'

For about thirty seconds she didn't move an inch. Then she calmly stood up, and walked out of the room. I followed, and found mum in her room, crying hysterically. I was in shock too. I felt as though I had just jumped from a very high building. I started crying as well and trying to talk to my mum. My brother and sister came into the room and tried to console the two of us.

After a while, everyone calmed down, and we could talk properly. It was so emotional. She said she was scared that I would be unhappy in life, and she felt embarrassed about other people knowing. She isn't homophobic, she just doesn't understand it. In fact, she is a feminist herself, and I got a lot of my beliefs and politics from her. She just can't comprehend the lesbian scene though, she thinks that some dykes have a male chauvinistic attitude.

I tried to convince her that I was happy, and my brother and sister supported me in this. My mum did tell one of her friends, who said that her own son was gay. This helped my mum to relax a bit. I bought her a book called *Different Daughters*, which she read and enjoyed.

Last time I saw her she said, 'I love you and I think you are very special.'

CLAIR, MINNEAPOLIS

Me and Geraldine had finally got it together on the Fourth of July, Independence Day, appropriately enough.

A couple of weeks later, I flew back to the States to see my family. Geraldine was my first woman and the whole thing seemed very new to me, so I didn't feel quite ready to come out at that stage.

However, our relationship was extremely passionate in those early days, and my neck was literally covered in huge red and purple lovebites. We'd tried to hold back for the few days preceding my trip, but you know how it is in the heat of the moment.

So there I am in ninety degrees of best USA sunshine, wearing polo-necks and little tasteful scarves. Of course my mom eventually sees, probably when I pass out from heatstroke, and asks me what on earth is wrong with my neck.

I affect my best attitude of casual nonchalance: 'Oh, something was in my bed in Belfast, some bug I guess.' It was the first time that Geraldine had been compared to an insect. My mom wanted to believe me, so we left it at that.

The years went by, and Geraldine and I were living together, and trying to have a child. I endeavoured to use this fact as a lead-in with my mom, by saying that I was keen to have a baby, and as I hadn't met a man that I wanted to share my life with, I might bring up my offspring with another woman. However, she didn't seem to take this idea very seriously and I knew it was time for a fresh angle.

I was getting fed up because each summer I visited, and each summer I left, with them none the wiser. They didn't really know about my life at all.

So, I decided to take the bull by the horns on a balmy August evening, as we were all sitting on the veranda. The conversation went something like this:

Me: Did I tell you that Geraldine and I have bought a car together?

Dad: Really? That's interesting. (huge pause)

Me: Did I tell you that Geraldine and I have opened a joint bank account?

Dad: Really? That's interesting. (bigger pause)

Me: Did I tell you that Geraldine and I share the same bed?

Dad: Well, you certainly have some good friends. (time stands still)

Me: (I take an enormously deep breath): I love Geraldine and she loves me.

Dad: Are you trying to tell me that this is a lesbian relationship?

Me: Yes that's exactly what I've been trying to tell you. I just haven't been succeeding.

He then said all the terrible, stereotypical things, it took about half an hour. But I think I've blocked them out because I love my dad so much. My parents were both unhappy and I cried for three days.

I was phoning Geraldine endlessly and sobbing into the receiver. I cried so much that I felt like my face was oozing liquid and was going to melt because my tears were so hot.

After three days I was completely dehydrated, and I took the only possible solution and went shopping. I returned home with new white trousers that were supposed to cheer me up, but were only succeeding in making me more miserable

My dad walked in with a huge smile on his face and offered to pay for my purchases. I don't know whether he was scared of losing me, or whether he just couldn't bear the next two weeks of the holiday being such a soggy affair.

But anyway, we were definitely friends again, and for the next two years I was number one perfect daughter. My sexuality was never mentioned, but besides that I couldn't put a foot wrong.

The third year, I took Geraldine to America, but it was a nightmare. Every time she walked into a room, my father walked out.

My sister rang and invited Geraldine to her wedding. My mother wrote and uninvited her. And so it went on.

I think my auntie really instigated the turning point. We were making sandwiches together one day, and she asked me if I'd be coming back next year for Grandaddy's ninetieth birthday party. I suddenly realized that I would be expected to come back year after year to 'family' gatherings, but my own family would never be included. Also I knew that the longer this went on for, the more difficult it would be to reverse people's presumptions – poor partnerless Clair. I wanted my relatives to at least acknowledge that I had my own life. I began to cry, tears running on to the sandwiches, and said that there was something I wanted to tell my auntie.

She replied that she knew, that my mother had told her, and then she said, 'If your parents aren't careful they're going to lose you completely.'

I couldn't believe it. Someone my mother's age was on my side. I was dumbfounded, and from that day onwards everything has been brilliant. My auntie's total acceptance had such a positive effect on my parents.

When Geraldine got pregnant, my mother was being really dodgy about everything, and saying terrible things like, 'You have no real relationship with her child.'

At this time, I know that my auntie decided to take charge. She sat my mother and father down and said, 'Do you want to lose your daughter? Because you're certainly going the right way about things. She is starting a family of her own now, and if you want to keep her in your family, you need to accept hers.'

This must have done the trick, because my parents are absolutely wonderful nowadays. Eventually, I think they would have got there themselves, but it would have taken a long time.

My auntie's so tuned in, she just made them see sense.

Imagine this, they were so keen to see Geraldine that they went on holiday via London. They absolutely adore her, she's the bee's knees. She's even in the family album.

The icing on the cake was when Mac, our son, was born. My mother rushed across the Atlantic, she said she couldn't wait to see her grandchild. Her saying that meant a lot to both of us.

Last year my mother was sixty. As a present, my dad arranged for all her children, and their children, to come over and surprise her. When the invitation arrived, addressed to 'Clair, Geraldine and Mac', I knew we'd finally made it.

HIDE-OUT

**Once I had a secret love,
that lived within the heart of me.
All too soon this secret love,
became impatient to be free.**

DORIS DAY

There's many an urban myth about the 'straight' man whose wife finds out about his uniform fetish when the local gay club is raided, and he arrives home in a bearskin at 3am.

However, the sad truth is that these 'double lives' cause a lot of pain and suffering. The people in this section seem glad that they managed to escape the foggy confusion and can see 'queerly' now.

GERALDINE, BELFAST

It was New Year's Eve 1986, and I decided that when I got back home to Belfast that night, I was going to tell my sister that

I was a lesbian. I had been having a serious relationship with a woman called Clair for some time. She was my first girlfriend, and I was hers. I knew that I had to tell everyone soon.

Up until then, my friends and family thought I was seeing a man called Keith, which was the identity I had substituted for Clair. Every time I mentioned 'Keith', it was really Clair I was talking about, but nobody knew. 'Keith' had a whole existence, a job and everything. Basically, I was pretending that Clair was a man.

I got completely drunk at the celebrations that night, and around midnight I realized that I really wanted to be in London with my woman. I told my companions that I needed to talk to my boyfriend, Keith, so we set off for the pub to use the pay-phone. Clair was in on her own when I phoned, so we were chatting away quite happily, when suddenly my friend Doreen yelled, 'Let me talk to Keith!' and snatched the receiver from my hand.

Clair obviously had to think quickly when she heard Doreen shrieking at her, so she said, 'Keith's just gone to get a cup of tea, I'm Clair, how are you?' I hurriedly brought the conversation to a close, casually said 'Goodbye' to Clair, and ushered my friends back to the house.

So there we were, drinking tea and chatting, mostly about 'Keith', although I did my best to steer the conversation on to other topics. All of a sudden, Doreen said, 'It's not Keith, it's Clair, isn't it?' I just nodded.

So that's how Doreen found out.

The night that Clair and I first got together was pretty spectacular too. Clair was actually working on a theatre project in Ireland at the time and I, funnily enough, was working in England. We were talking every night on the phone, till at least 5am. It was a kind of vocal courtship. We were falling in love but pretending to be just good friends.

On the opening night of Clair's show, I decided to fly back and surprise her. We were delighted to see each other, but still deceiving ourselves about our true feelings. Later that evening, I was sitting in quite a rough pub, with a big group of people, and Clair walked through the door. To my surprise, she pushed past all my friends to get to me, said, 'I love you, Geraldine Caldwell,' and snogged me in front of everyone.

I replied, 'And I love you too, Clair Chapman.'

We've been together for ten years so far.

RAY, CROYDON

It was during the mid 1970s that I began to come out. Locally, there was so much activity. There was a **CHE** branch [The Campaign for Homosexual Equality], there were regular Saturday night lesbian and gay discos, and **Gay News** and **Sappho** were available.

I started to meet others, not just to chat them up and have sex, but to talk about the 'gay community' which was quite a new concept for me. I began to discuss issues like 'pride' and 'coming out'; to campaign against discrimination, and to raise funds by organizing jumble sales.

I went to meetings and heard speakers from the **Gay Liberation Front**. It was fun and exciting, it changed my life. Suddenly I began to take an interest in gay politics, and to think about our unwritten history. For the first time, I became aware of the oppression we had silently suffered. I made many new friends.

I realized that this was a time of great importance for all of us. It was as if a burden was being lifted. Looking back, I don't know who coined the phrase 'coming out'. But whoever they were, they provided a concept which struck a chord in every gay person's mind. This was to alter our lives completely. None of us could ever be the same again.

Before I 'came out', I spent most of my life in fear and panic trying not to be 'found out', I can clearly remember how skilfully I deceived my family, friends and workmates, to ensure that they didn't discover the 'other' me.

There were two compartments in my life: one contained the role I played for the straight world, the other was full of the experiences and attitudes I'd gained from my secret excursions into the 'queer zone'.

My double life continued from my early teens until I was forty-two. I think that some of the uneasiness of this period still exists, and affects the way I am today. A really straight event can trigger flutterings in my stomach, which make me feel insecure. These strange feelings are probably the remains of my past fear of being found out. Even I think that this is odd after so many years of being out.

The heated debates of the 1970s always centred on the need to feel pride in the personal struggles that were taking place. This certainly wasn't easy for me. I had experienced a lifetime of ducking and diving, of avoiding being honest. I had learnt to accept the verdict of others: people who described me as unnatural, perverted and not to be trusted with children.

Now I had to massively readjust my feelings about myself, and assess where I was. I needed to ditch all the negative images and find positive alternatives.

I didn't want to come out as a terrified queen. I wanted to be self-confident and feel worthwhile. I no longer wanted to be frightened of who I was. I wanted to be proud. This was no easy task. My expectations exceeded the personal strength and political resources available to me at the time. I worked hard to achieve my aims, much still has to be completed. Sensibly, I soon realized that it was an endless project.

I was helped tremendously by articles I read, and I enjoyed lots of debates. There were many divisions along the way. On one side there were the 'nice' gay men who wanted the process to slow down and to avoid anything which might be considered to be 'political'. On the other side were the gays from the 'left'. They wanted action which was direct, assertive and uncompromising.

In retrospect, I think that the diffidence of the 'nice' men, who couldn't quite come out of the closet, sabotaged much of the impact of the early years of gay liberation. We had to learn that our community was a diverse beast. I used to think that we only had one common denominator: our homosexual desire. However, I came to realize that more important things united us: oppression and discrimination, which were suffered by all.

I felt that it was time for my theories to be put into practice; I should actually try and come out to someone.

The first person was Christine. She was straight and married, but luckily a feminist. The momentous occasion took place in a coffee shop at Sloane Square. I'd been giving her advice about her troubled marriage, and, just before we left, I told her that I was gay. She didn't seem surprised. She was kindly about the news and said that it didn't make any difference to her. She did know other men who were gay, but I was the first one who had actually come out to her.

On the bus home I felt pleased. I'd done it. I'd told someone. I was in control, I'd taken the initiative. I'd been brave.

However, a new worry suddenly struck me. I trusted Christine, and liked her, but would she tell others? I hadn't asked her not to, I just presumed she'd realize that my sexuality wasn't common knowledge. What if she told my boss? Would he be difficult? I needed to sort it out in my own time, and not feel obliged to face everyone at once. As it turned out, I was unnecessarily anxious. Christine was the soul of discretion until I was ready to tell more people.

After my first coming out I felt good. I wondered if I should have done it earlier. However, I realized that, psychologically, it would not have been possible sooner. I needed the support of my local CHE group, their activities and debates. People there had inspired me and I had done a lot of earnest thinking. Many factors had come together and influenced my ideas about who 'we' were and who 'we' could become. Since the 1970s, much of my life has centred around working in the lesbian and gay community. The emergence of the visible ghetto has meant that much of my social life is spent with other homosexuals, and in exclusively gay gatherings.

All my family know that I'm gay and it doesn't appear to have made much difference. I've lived in the same street for twenty years, most of my neighbours know and are fine about it.

After all these years, I no longer feel the need to come out directly when I meet new people. Usually something comes up in the conversation that confirms my gay status.

If a young person asked me about coming out, my advice would be to come out to yourself fully first, and then move the process on to other people. Along the way, read everything that you can get your hands on, everything about *our* history. Be informed and talk about it. Find out what it will mean for you and others.

We are now into the second generation of gay people coming out. It has stood the test of time and is still a very powerful thing to do.

STEPHEN, BRISTOL

I was living in Morecambe and I was unhappy. This was partly because I was living in Morecambe, but mainly because I knew I was gay, and had decided I didn't want to be. I didn't really like myself very much.

The answer seemed obvious at the time: I created a whole new persona for myself.

The new Stephen was crazy and wild, the life and soul of the party. He took drugs and was noisy, loud and disruptive. He liked hanky-panky and skylarking games. Anything that would distract me from my true feelings, I jumped upon. This facade seemed so much more appealing than what I knew to be inside. For a long time I believed in this charade myself. It became a smoke-screen for me as much as for anyone else.

Eventually, of course, the power of my true sexuality broke through and I had to acknowledge it. The force of real feelings was too strong to deny. That night I sat my girlfriend down. 'Julie,' I said, 'I've got something to tell you . . .'

She was incredibly supportive and encouraged me to tell my friends, who were also brilliant. They thought that it was fascinating and that I was brave.

It was curious really, because part of my adopted persona had been to be very laddish. So, out of my peer group, I was probably the one least expected to turn out queer. A lot of people had to adjust their impression of me.

I think that my current behaviour, which is straight-acting, is largely attributable to this type of role-playing. I like the acceptability of being one of the crowd and not being seen as queer. I have tremendous admiration for camp people and those who are overtly and recognizably gay.

I found telling my friends to be such an affirming experience. I was suddenly the centre of attention, not because of my stupid antics, but because of my homosexuality. It was inspiring, and; in a heaving rush, I decided to come out to my parents.

I didn't want to tell them over the phone, so I waited till I went home for the holidays. It was a very droll experience.

Safely in the parental nest, I began the weekend:

Me: Mum, I hope you don't mind if I have the odd cigarette around the house, because I smoke these days.

Mum: What, *funny* cigarettes?

It wasn't what I'd meant at all, but because I was so psyched up to make revelations to them, I just said, 'Yes.'

So that night began with them already in a state of shock. We were having a trauma, but it wasn't the one I'd planned. My coming out was being upstaged.

My father then decided that he needed to try some dope, 'to see what all the fuss is about'.

Half an hour later, we were all sitting around the family hearth with my dad puffing on a bong pipe. He was getting progressively stoned, and saying things like, 'Well I'm not affected by this at all,' and then making really stupid jokes, giggling a lot, and eating every biscuit in the house. My mum just watched, looking perplexed.

It was a bizarre situation because at that time they thought that dope led to heroin which led to death.

I was completely wound up about telling them I was queer, and I couldn't wait any longer. So I just came out with it, so to speak. It was a very explosive moment. They were fabulous, but it was obvious that they felt their world was crumbling. Their youngest son was not only a drug addict, but gay as well. However, they are Quakers, so could not condemn me overtly. They were just totally uncomprehending.

Their response was to try and find out more about it. From the very first moment there were questions, not comments. They wanted to know whether it was caused or inborn; questions I couldn't even answer now. I wasn't very helpful really because I was feeling so insecure about it all myself. I was trying to be defiant, but I actually had no confidence in my sexuality. We were all negotiating it together.

In the end, however, I think it brought us closer together, because ultimately they were glad that I felt I could tell them. We now share a mutual trust, which is very special.

My coming out has always been a personalized internal process. Nobody has ever confronted me with it from outside and said, 'I think you're a poof.'

I'm lucky because I've done it on my own terms. However, I get frustrated with the continual process of coming out. I'm still not very good at it. Sometimes I blush and stammer while I'm telling people, and then I get annoyed with myself. It gives the impression that I'm not at ease with my sexuality, which I am. Politically, I think it's important to present a confident, assertive image of a gay man.

To tell the truth, I would like to be more camp. This type of image has such strength and honesty. I feel deeply uncomfortable in a room, socially or professionally, with people who don't know I'm queer. I don't feel a necessity to tell casual acquaintances at a cocktail party. However, people I have any type of relationship with have to know, it's such an important part of me. I would never want anyone to think that I was hiding it, or feeling ashamed of my sexuality. I'm proud of my partner, and I love the fact that he is as camp as a row of pink tents. I adore taking him to business functions. He outs us both as I walk in with him on my arm.

My neurotic fixation with coming out has been hugely helped by my involvement with activism. You don't need to 'tell' someone if they've seen a photograph of you being arrested at an **OutRage!** demonstration in the *Independent on Sunday*.

When this particular picture was in the press, I got a flurry of phone calls from business associates. They respected what I was doing, even if they didn't really understand it.

I hold quite an important position in my chosen field, which is photography, and this has been invaluable. I am very proud of the fact that I have managed to educate and inform others who are influential in this area of the media. I think that a lot of my colleagues now treat queer issues with more respect than they would otherwise have done. This is one area where my coming out has had wide-reaching consequences and hopefully been very constructive.

CAUGHT OUT

**Anguish of all sizes . . .
millions of surprises.**

A.P. HERBERT

The people in this section have all had experiences of unplanned coming out. These can be the tricky ones as you haven't had time to prepare your speech, let alone check your hair. Sometimes, being discovered and exposed can be a relief, but that depends on what you're doing at the time . . .

AMIT, BOLTON

My coming out was a surprise for all involved. Mum was away for the day, and due back late. Me and Tom were in bed having a post-fuck smoke. Hearing a noise, I totally panicked. As the door swung open I quickly handed Tom my cigarette. Mum walked straight in. So now she knows I'm queer, but at least she doesn't know I smoke.

KAY, LONDON

I have never said anything directly to my mother about my sexuality, but I'm sure that she is well aware of my lesbian status. I haven't had a relationship with a man for seven years, but she's had a stronger hint than that. I got very drunk at my sister's graduation, phoned my girlfriend, and told her that if she came to pick me up, I'd take her home and shag her brains out. I didn't realize that my mum was standing next to the phone.

Later, she apparently said to her friend, 'I just don't understand why her girlfriend didn't take her up on it, it seemed like such a good offer.'

Other than that, we've never discussed it.

When I was about fourteen, I was well aware of what I really wanted, but I didn't do anything about it until I was sixteen when I had a brief fling with a girl at school. That was a passionate relationship but it ended badly.

At college I was going out with a man, but I never had sex with him because I only wanted women. I told him that, and strangely enough he didn't seem bothered. Eventually I fell in love with a woman, and we stayed together for three years.

A few groups at college, like the rugby club for instance, were pretty homophobic. In the end I went to the pub with them, drank them all under the table, and soon altered their opinions of lesbians. I got a bit of respect after that. At the time I was sleeping with the girlfriend of the team captain, so I think that may have caused some of the antagonism. Especially when she finished with him to go out with me.

Even though I was out at college, I still felt deep down that it was wrong. I felt insulted to be called a lesbian. It's only really in the last six months that I've been confident about it.

The trouble is that no one ever explains anything at school. When you're going through puberty and your hormones are all over the place, the last thing you need to be told is, 'Silly girl, it's just a phase.'

Teenagers should be reassured that it's not the greatest sin in the world, that there are positive role models, and that it's not a phase.

SAMANTHA, BIRMINGHAM

I belong to a group that dresses up in traditional costume and re-enacts battles. There was a woman in my regiment who found out I was lesbian from somebody else. I heard that she was upset with me, so I took her to one side and asked her what the problem was. She said she was hurt that I hadn't told her myself.

I said to her, 'In all the time we've worked together, have you ever come and told me that you are heterosexual?'

She got the point.

FREAKING OUT

**There is nothing to be guilty of,
our love is one in a million.**

BARBRA STREISAND

It is common for lesbians and gay men to feel that they have let their family down, and feel terribly guilty as a consequence. Parents sometimes blame themselves for their child's sexuality: 'Where did I go wrong? I knew we shouldn't have bought him those bunny slippers . . .'

Guilt is an unproductive emotion and achieves little. Our community needs individuals who feel positive about themselves in order to be able to work towards the future.

DAVID, SOUTH SHIELDS

We were all quite drunk. It had been such a great night. I'd been working with one of my mum's heroes, Helen Shapiro, and I'd managed to introduce them. She was over the moon, and I felt my Brownie points were high.

I had a scheme worked out, to bring the issue on to the agenda, to make them acknowledge what I was sure they already knew. I took them to an Italian restaurant and the Frascati was flowing freely:

Me: Sometimes I feel as if you don't love me.

Them: Of course we do, son.

Me: But you never ask about my life. I wonder if you care sometimes.

100

Them: Of course we care.

Me: Do you?

Them: Yes. We worry about you all the time.

Me: Why do you worry?

Them: You know why.

Me: Well, that's just how I am and I'm happy.

Mum: But I don't want you to be old and lonely, and have a Pekinese on your arm when you're fifty.

Having said this, my mum broke down and began to sob.

We talked. They were worried about AIDS. So I tried to be reassuring; telling them that I was a healthy young man who was 'careful'. We were talking in euphemisms. My mum was crying quite voraciously by now, her tears splashing on to her tagliatelle alfredo. She only ever ate alfredo. Dad seemed to be on the sidelines, but he kept saying he cared.

I started reeling off this massive list of people that mum liked or admired; famous people and friends of mine. I didn't say they were gay, the word seemed to have a sharp edge to it. I just said that they were 'like me'. More euphemisms. We were practically speaking in code.

Mum also seemed anxious that other people had known before her. Had they been laughing behind her back because she had a gay son?

We talked around the issues for a while. When the situation seemed calmer, I drove them back to their B&B.

That night, I felt totally overjoyed and elated. I'd done it. Yes it had been traumatic, but it could have been worse. I'd come out, and the only way from here was up. I was so looking forward to being close to my mum again. As a teenager I had such a good relationship with her. We used to be really open and discuss our sex lives. At the time, I was the envy of my school friends. I wanted so badly to rediscover our intimacy.

When I went to pick them up the next morning, I stated my

hopes in a very simple way:

Me: I'm so glad that we had that conversation last night.

Mum: I'm not glad.

Me: What?

Mum: I don't want to talk about it any more. Ever.

I felt as if a steel barrier came down between us at that moment. Seven years later it is still there. It divides us, so that even when we shout, the words are still muffled, and we can't hear each other properly.

Telling my parents was a desperate need. I didn't want to live falsely. Their reaction has deeply affected my confidence. It's like a weak link in my armour. Because of them, I still carry huge guilt about my sexuality. People accepting you gives you strength.

I keep toying with the idea of saying, 'Accept me, or fuck off.'

But ultimately, I'm too scared to do this in case they say, 'OK, we'll go.' Permanently. And then I'd be even more of an emotional wreck. Or would I?

If we did separate, I also think that my mother might turn the situation around – she's quite good at that – and say: 'See, I knew I'd given birth to an evil child. He's rejected me.'

We keep passing the guilt back and forth. I feel bad because of the money they invested in me when I was younger. I'd like to earn loads of money in my career, to prove to them that you can be successful and gay. Then I'd pay them back with all this homosexually tainted cash. I'd like to throw it at them as revenge. But would they take it? Perhaps they'd think that if they accepted the dosh, they'd be under obligation to accept me. Love my money, love me.

I constantly wish that their reaction was better. I used to think that it was all my fault, but at least I think of it as their problem now. I feel very hurt by what's happened, and I punish my parents by only going to see them when I want. This pain brings out the child in me.

Perhaps if I was in a long-term relationship, things would be easier. The nebulous quality of my sexuality would suddenly be physicalized as 'someone'. Maybe a charming and gentle man who would win them over. It's a Catch-22 situation though, I'm so fucked up by them that I find it difficult to sustain a long-term relationship. I seem to commit to men who are very wrong for me. And when someone is giving me what I want, I panic and run away. The lack of acceptance from my parents has left me emotionally scarred. This makes me very angry, and I don't want to end up bitter.

IAN, WORTHING

I remember when I was a child, rubbing up against my father's legs and loving the feeling of hairiness. I was four years old then, and I've had a thing about hairy legs ever since.

I first came out while at sixth form college. I was sitting in the canteen with three friends and we were telling secrets. I was toying with the idea of saying, 'My secret is that I'm a triplet.' But everyone knew that anyway. So when it came to my turn I just said, 'I sleep with men.'

This was received in stunned silence, probably because their secrets were so boring by comparison. The effect it had on me, though, was far greater. Saying it out loud just blew me apart. It made me realize fully what I was about, and that there was no choice in the matter.

The first thing I did after this was to ask a girl out! She has since turned out to be a lesbian, which is interesting. I think it is quite common for gay men and lesbians to go out together while discovering their sexuality.

I realized soon afterwards that I would have to tell my parents. I was pretty screwed up at this stage and felt that I could never be myself unless I actually said to my mother and father, 'I am gay.' I suspected that one of my elder brothers might also be gay. I still do; thirty-five and not married? Bit of a dead give-away I think. However, the other two triplets are straight; so much for the gay gene.

Anyway, after a visit to the Brighton Gay Youth Group, which was a very positive experience, I wrote my parents a letter. It was pretty apologetic, I kept saying that it wasn't their fault that I was a poof. I stated that this was me, there was no changing it, and it was just bad luck. I left the letter on the sideboard and went out.

I was shitting myself all day, and when I returned that evening, only my dad was in. He was obviously distraught and he called me up to his room. He said he wanted to talk about the letter. I said, 'What about it?' He replied, 'Your mother's very upset.'

I always remember that, because I felt so guilty about it, but my mother never mentioned it, not for many years. I've asked her since if she ever suspected, given the fact that I was deeply unhappy throughout my teenage years. She says she didn't, which I find a bit hurtful. Could she not guess? I mean, I played with dolls until the age of fifteen.

At the age of eighteen, I had a huge crush on a guy at college. He was butch, beautiful, well-built – and straight. I adored him and he knew it. I wanted to be like him. In fact, he was so into Dire Straits that I bought all their albums. What a load of old crap! I've got rid of them now, of course. I think I might even have burnt one.

GREG, IRELAND

My mum blamed herself, and reminded me of an event that had happened in the early 1980s.

When I was fifteen, she had invited my girlfriend to stay the night, in the spare room. In the early hours she had caught me creeping across the landing and had gone mad. She had severely reprimanded me, saying that I had betrayed her trust and that I was far too young to be considering a sexual relationship with my girlfriend.

Years on, she looked at her grown gay son and burst into tears: 'Why did I stop you sneaking into your girlfriend's room?' she sobbed, 'I wish I'd encouraged you now.'

I know that her encouragement wouldn't have made any difference in the long run, but I can't seem to make her realize this. Sometimes I think she looks back over my childhood wondering if she 'made mistakes' along the way.

I gently point out that she brought me and my two brothers up in exactly the same manner, and they seem to be very well-adjusted, happy heterosexuals. I believe that I was born this way and that my mother had absolutely nothing to do with it.

I think the older generations are particularly worried that they may somehow aid the development of a homosexual. I know that my grandad thought it was very important that any such tendencies were nipped in the bud.

My brother used to like trying on my sister's nurse's uniform and pushing the cat round the garden in a pram. I remember my grandad seeing this sight one summer's afternoon, and nearly fainting. When he recovered, he told my mum that she should prevent such activities, and that she must be firmer with us. So perhaps her guilt is inherited.

Part Two

Shouting Out

IMAGE

Express yourself.

MADONNA

So, you've come out, either to yourself or those around you. The years of guilt, worry and fancying your best friend are behind you. What happens next?

Everyone I spoke to agreed that coming out was the beginning of a new phase in their lives. Suddenly there were opportunities to embrace, and a personal freedom that wasn't there before. Some people changed their behaviour or their appearance; lesbians cut their hair, gay men started using large amounts of styling gel. Some went wild on the gay scene, some came out to everyone they knew, some told the milkman, some *had* the milkman.

ZOE, LONDON

I felt huge relief when I'd come out to my mother and rushed out to buy a **labrys** necklace. But you have to excuse me because I was young, and I didn't wear it for long. It's very embarrassing to look back on my labrys experience. I wouldn't be seen dead in one now. I didn't feel the necessity to alter my appearance in any other way because I already looked like a dyke. I'd had very short hair and eighteen-hole docs for years.

LUCY, MANCHESTER

Since I was small I've had very long, blonde hair. By the time I came out, it was almost waist-length.

I had it cropped. Right off. It was such a liberating experience. I think it made my parents see me in a new light as well. They couldn't pretend I was still a little girl unable to make her own decisions.

This was a new Lucy with sleek, short hair and a lesbian lover.

TAM, CAMDEN

I used to have long, blonde locks before I came out. Once my sexuality was established and I felt more confident, I cut it all off to look like a stereotypical dyke. I wanted to make a statement that I was gay and loved it. It didn't end with the haircut, I stopped wearing skirts and being feminine too. Now I wear big boots and jeans and feel completely happy and comfortable. I would like to give up my office job and start doing manual work.

MAXINE, PRESTON

I went away to college in a new town. It was a fresh start and finally I had the strength to be me – the person I had always wanted to be.

I was such an out lesbian. Instantly recognizable. I came to university wearing my Brighton dyke-scene uniform: a skinhead, black leather and white Levi T-shirt. Perhaps Preston wasn't ready for this. The very first day, I was walking through town and a man came up to me and poked his finger in my chest, saying; 'We don't want fucking dykes like you here.'

However, it had its compensations. At our very first lecture, three lesbians walked in, looked around and headed straight for me. We're all still friends today.

I'm very empowered by looking like a dyke. I don't mind being a walking stereotype. I like playing around with my image. If people think that I look like a man, that's their problem. I don't feel like a man. I love women and I want other dykes to know that.

Another very out thing I did was to 'marry' my girlfriend, Louise. We had been friends before we became partners, and we wanted people to take our relationship seriously. We organized a commitment ceremony and invited all our friends. We designed some rings, copyrighted the pattern and had them made by a jeweller. They're yin and yang and fit together perfectly.

Nobody in Preston would come along and bless us, so we just said how much we loved each other and exchanged rings. That was two years ago. It was quite a brave thing to do, because my partner is not out in other areas of her life.

When I was younger, I would have had a definite problem with this. I used to go around saying that all my partners had to be completely out. It was my radical lesbian politics, but now I realize that this is not always possible. Being involved with Louise has helped me get certain things in perspective. I am helping to raise her son and that is a priority. Nothing must threaten that.

KAY, LONDON

The first summer at university, I shaved all my hair off and got my nose pierced. This was definitely a dyke statement and I'm looking to getting more body parts pierced in the future.

I plan to foster children at some point in my life. Ideally, I would like to care for young people coming to terms with their sexuality.

JO, HERTFORDSHIRE

Three years ago I decided to have my hair cut short. It was partly as a statement but more because my girlfriend said it would suit me. It didn't. I hated it, so now I have a bob. There seems to be a bob movement amongst lesbians at the moment. It's nice to know I was there first!

SUSAN, WINKLEIGH

When I first began living as an out gay person, I really went for it with my 'lesbian appearance'. I had the full works: no hair, big boots, leather jacket and lots of piercings. I was lucky to be in a theatre company at the time, and in that environment it's OK to have no hair and nine earrings. Basically, I could look any way I wanted to, and I chose to look like a lesbian. Also, loads of women seemed to fancy me, I was getting picked up all the time. Lots of sex. Now I've changed my image a bit and I have a bob and lipstick. I've come through the stage of saying 'being a lesbian is my identity', and now I feel that being a lesbian is part of me, but it's not everything.

I work in broadcasting, but I've never applied to a gay programme. I don't want to live in a ghetto, I want to compete on the same platform as everyone else in television. Having said that, I do believe that gay people's sense of community is very important. I feel strongly about issues that affect lesbians and gay men, and I think that more of us should get involved in fighting for gay rights.

MELANIE, EDINBURGH

I had no intention of changing my image when I came out. My mother, however, had other ideas. She didn't care who I was sleeping with, but she began to cry because she thought I was going to shave my head. No way. I love my slick bob. It's smart and adaptable. It means I can choose who to tell about my sexuality. It isn't being shouted from the rooftops before I even open my mouth. I wouldn't want an image that says, 'Here comes a lesbian'. I want people to think, 'Here comes Melanie'. And the rest is up to me.

BECKY, KENDAL

As soon as I was out of the closet I cut my hair off. I changed what I was wearing too, mainly for practical reasons. You can't really be Miss Floaty Skirt at Greenham. Nowadays, I don't adopt such a dykey image. I don't feel the need to. There is more diversity in our community now.

MARTIN, PUTNEY

There are definitely certain jobs that homosexuals gravitate towards, which then develop an image of being predominantly gay. I'm sure that a million gay men became shop assistants because of John Inman in *Are You Being Served?* It frightens me to think that they did, but what can you do?

I'm convinced that many gay people go into the caring professions because they can relate so well to the clients they deal with. They understand what it feels like to be told that you are doing the wrong thing all the time, that you are not conforming as society wants you to. Gay people can identify with anyone who is being made to feel that they are abnormal. Those already working in the caring professions are less likely to be judgemental, which also makes it an attractive career for queers. There is a smaller chance of experiencing homophobia than, say, in an accountancy firm, where generally people are only too willing to put you down.

RISHMA, EAST AFRICA

When I admitted that I was a lesbian, I became far more confident. Before that I had always worn nasty glasses and tried to hide my face. I used to act butch the whole time and swagger around. After I came out to myself, I felt more like a full woman, I stopped behaving like a boy. I felt able to celebrate my femininity, I'm sure I looked more attractive.

I loved the dyke scene at first, I felt I had discovered a whole new world where I fitted in, a secure, safe place where I belonged. I went to gay clubs and bars every day. On the lesbian scene, people seemed to find me attractive. Before that I had always felt like the ugly one that no one wanted to go out with. Basically, I discovered the joy of women's company.

ACTIVISM

What am I going to do with all this anger?

MADONNA

For many lesbian and gay people, activism can be an outlet for fury and frustration. Becoming actively involved in the gay rights movement can also give a great feeling of solidarity, of a community working together to bring about change. Many people describe their experiences in direct action as 'empowering', and say that taking part gave them added confidence in their own sexuality. It's also a fantastic natural high and a great way of meeting people . . .

ANTHONY, ABERGAVENNY

When I was out and had moved to the city, I got involved in quite a lot of activism. Even though I don't go to so many meetings any more, I do still consider myself to be an activist.

I'm always ready to put my oar in if I think something needs to be said. It leads to a lot of arguments, but I think it's worth it.

I don't believe in outing, though, except in the case of hypocrites who are gay but slag off other queers. I'm into reclaiming language, and I always call myself a poof before someone else can.

TAM, CAMDEN

Joining the **Lesbian Avengers** has completely changed my life. It has made me more politically aware and able to do some-

113

thing positive for lesbian rights. The thrill of activism is wonderful. It has also given me an amazing social life!

FISCH, LONDON

At twenty-four, I went to Greenham Common for the first time. It was there I realized that I could celebrate my sexuality. I had nothing to feel guilty about. It was a revelation. I had gone for a weekend and ended up staying a year and a half. Greenham changed my life and saved it as well. I managed to get off intravenous drugs while I was there.

The most amazing action we did was a naked blockade of the main entrance. We all took our clothes off, smeared ourselves with mud and fake blood, then lay down in front of the gate. When the guards saw us they completely freaked out. They didn't know what to do and simply stood staring. I found it incredibly empowering and pretty ironic that these straight men, used to getting off on naked women, were actually too terrified to touch us.

We lay there for an hour while tourists drove past trying to hide their children's eyes. After that, a troop of women guards appeared wearing gloves, and dragged us away. They put us in a van and drove this busload of naked women to Newbury Jail. They only released us when we agreed to put on the Salvation Army clothes that they provided. There wasn't one pair of trousers in the bag, so we were all freed wearing nylon A-line skirts. The whole experience was hysterical and it taught me the power of my own body. Without activism, I think it would have taken me far longer to come to terms with my sexuality and to feel strong.

However, a few years later I was at a demonstration outside the South African Embassy. I was arrested for throwing brussels sprouts, and put into a van. The policemen cuffed my hands behind my back and one of them began hitting me. I was absolutely terrified, but I managed to spit in his face. When I arrived at the police station I already had a black eye. The police doctor refused to take my complaint seriously and said I had no proof. I felt powerless. I stopped doing direct action after that.

JO, HERTFORDSHIRE

I call myself a woman activist rather than a feminist. I don't feel that feminism relates to me or to my life. After I had been out for a while, I got really fed up going to lesbian groups that were discussion-based. Hours can be spent talking about oppression, and nothing is achieved. I joined the Lesbian Avengers thinking that they intended to go out and take action. They do, and I love it.

STEVE, GEORGIA

I have a tremendous amount of respect for activists. I think their actions have got a lot of people to pay attention where they otherwise wouldn't. There are some situations where the regular channels for getting things done just don't work.

In America, technically, there is no place where two men can have sex and be within their legal rights. Every state has sodomy laws. In Virginia, it's even illegal for a woman to be on top of a man during sex.

There was a case in Georgia recently, where a policeman was tracking a robber in a certain neighbourhood. While sneaking around the back of a house, he looked through a window and saw two men having sex. He abandoned the chase, and arrested the two men for sodomy. They took their case to the Supreme Court and lost. A group of gay ex-servicemen arranged a huge demonstration at the court, asking why they had fought for their country only to find that it provides them with no rights.

There are many religious groups in America who believe that AIDS isn't the issue, it is the answer. Things in the States are starting to get scary. I think that by the year 2000, we will be tattooed at best and lynched at worst. People there are using AIDS as an excuse to take away gay civil rights, saying that it is the Lord's punishment for sin. We have to oppose these people in any way we can.

ISLA, LONDON

The best thing about being an activist is kicking the butts of the straights and telling it the way it is. Not standing for any shit is good fun.

STEPHEN, BRISTOL

I'm involved in activism for several reasons. I'm aware that not everyone has had the opportunities and privileges that I've had, like supportive parents and colleagues. I want to hold up a banner for other queers to follow, to show them how much is possible.

Activism, and OutRage! in particular, is an oppositional force. It's about saying: we will not tolerate oppression, we do not accept this particular bit of legislation. It's a voice shouting, 'No, fuck off,' and being offensively assertive.

It's so important, because, looking back over the history of the queer rights movement, people will not give anything if you are 'nice'. The same has been true with black civil rights, the women's movement, and many other groups. I think it's particularly pertinent to queer equality because there is such a psychological fear surrounding the subject. Direct action is good at forcing people to address issues, because you have embarrassed them into it.

Being involved in OutRage! you come face to face with antagonism. The group is shunned and hated by some.

I feel as if I was crippled throughout my adolescence and my twenties by the desire to be liked and accepted by all. I now feel that my peers in OutRage! and my partner, Robert, have given me the strength to accept that in certain circumstances, if you believe in what you're doing, it's OK not to be liked.

In fact, I get suspicious if people like what OutRage! is doing too much. It makes me think that we must be going wrong somewhere and are not being strong enough.

If my peers in the lesbian and gay community don't agree with what I'm doing, I think it is an evangelical mission to persuade them. I believe that I'm speaking for them, but a lot of people won't understand. This is because there are no immediate results from what we do, but there are very definitely long-term effects.

I don't claim to represent any wider constituency than those people who come along to OutRage! However, I do feel that we are benefiting a much wider community, and if they don't like it, they should try and do something about it.

LOLA, MASSACHUSETTS

I was too young to participate in the black movement, but it taught me that people can make a difference. There isn't anyone like Martin Luther King or Malcolm X today, and there is still racism in the world.

Being in **ACT UP** in the late 1980s was a hugely positive experience for me. Even though the gay movement is younger, I think that it has had more success. I attribute this to the fact that, if you're black, the whole world can see, whereas if you're gay you can always choose to go back in the closet.

STEVEN, LANCASHIRE

I would describe myself as a shy activist. Occasionally this makes it difficult to take part in some of OutRage!'s more brazen activities. Such in-your-face behaviour doesn't come naturally to me. My camera somehow legitimizes my presence. It offers me a defence against the world, and makes me feel much more confident.

This is something I have seen with a lot of photographers: take their cameras away and they become a mass of jelly. I think it is a common phenomenon.

The most terrifying and therefore the most exhilarating action I've ever been involved in was the Michael Haimes **zap**. He is Director for Public Prosecutions, and is responsible for **Operation Spanner**. This was my scariest protest for two reasons. In my mind I had built Haimes into a bogeyman of such power and authority – which indeed he is – that I'd become totally intimidated by him. Secondly, we had to sit in a public meeting for four hours waiting for him to speak. We effectively became absorbed into the group, and I was even chatting away to the nun next to me.

As the meeting progressed, I became more terrified of disrupting the social order there, and of confronting this bogeyman. The waiting was more frightening than the action, but we had to blend in at this point to be successful, which we were.

Afterwards, I bumped into my nun again. She turned out to be a fab woman, very pro-queer!

SARIT, ISRAEL

Activism is something that I can't do without. I didn't choose it, it is just necessary to my life. I can't sit back and let bad things happen, I guess that's why I'm a Lesbian Avenger.

KATHERINE, LONDON

When I was twenty-four and having my first relationship, I didn't know there was such a thing as Pride. The lesbian scene was a strange mixture then. It was the tail end of 1970s feminism with all its strict rules about how to behave, while the bar scene was pretty wild and apolitical.

I went to the last **Lesbian Strength** march in 1988, where lesbian feminism completely died, if I remember. Soon after, I started work as the office girl for the **Pink Paper**. It was there that I started noticing what was going on around me, and began thinking about activism.

I got very involved in the **SM** argument, as I couldn't understand how people could condemn it when they wore all the gear! I actually gave a speech at a debate in favour of SM sex, merely because I thought it was the right thing to do. As a result, I was befriended for life by a huge group of leather-clad SM dykes. After that, if ever they saw me they would whoop and cheer, while my lesbian feminist friends would politely ask, 'Katherine, do you know those people?'

My first real experience of activism was through OutRage! The Lesbian and Gay Christian Movement had tipped me off that OutRage! were doing something exciting on Sunday morning at Westminster Cathedral. So, full of enthusiasm, I made myself a placard and went along. I walked into the church and scoured the congregation for homosexuals, but I could see none. Then I spotted **Peter Tatchell** sidling along a pew and I realized that this was probably an undercover operation. Feeling suddenly conspicuous in the centre aisle holding a huge banner, I ran outside, snapped the stick off my placard, hid it, and crept back into the cathedral.

About ten minutes into the service, a man in a suit walked calmly up to the front, took the microphone and said, 'Do not be alarmed. This is an OutRage! action.'

Suddenly, people materialized from all parts of the church, walked to the front and held up their banners. I was stunned. I just thought, 'How amazing, how slick, how incredibly well organized.' Before I knew it, I found myself walking towards the front to join them. They must have thought, 'who the hell is she?' but luckily I had my best T-shirt on, which read: 'God is an equal opportunities employer. Pity about the church.'

Eventually we were ushered out, and I stood outside with the other OutRage! members, distributing leaflets and explaining what we were doing. Nobody asked me who I was. I think they were just glad of the support. That was my first OutRage! action. I've been hooked ever since!

BECKY, KENDAL

The best action I participated in at Greenham was the invasion of the silos. The guards were armed and we thought they might shoot at us. I had to argue to be allowed to take part, because I was so young, but I was very passionate about wanting to do it and the group eventually gave in.

We climbed over the fence and started running towards the silos. We managed to get on top of them and stayed there for about an hour. It was so brilliant and I felt really positive and empowered by it all. After that, there were articles in the local paper about me, saying how I had run off to Greenham and got arrested. They never said I was a lesbian though.

I don't think that something like Greenham could really happen today. People's goals seem to be smaller and we have new restrictions on peaceful protest from the **Criminal Justice Act** to contend with.

KAY, LONDON

I just love the idea of direct action which is why I had to join Lesbian Avengers. My ideal demonstration would be to zap the Queen.

SALLY, GLAMORGAN

I believe in direct action and fighting for our rights in public. However, the most radical action is coming out to your neighbour, or your boss, or your grandmother. Sooner or later, almost everyone will know a gay person, and that process will really bring about change.

STEVEN, IRELAND

Once I'd come out I was rather desperate for boyfriends. But I was in Lancaster, which didn't seem particularly rich in them.

I think I needed someone to help me consolidate my new sexuality, some sort of sexual affirmation, but the men weren't exactly queuing up.

I dabbled in cruising and cottaging but I've never felt confident about public sex. I preferred to operate in bars and clubs, and did have a few casual partners. Ultimately though, I never found it satisfying, I wanted to have some form of relationship. However cursory the encounter, I needed to know their names.

I would then get frustrated with this lifestyle, and go into a period of celibacy, thinking that it wasn't worth the anguish. But then the sexual pressure would build up and I'd go out and have two or three flings. These would be boring, pointless and embarrassing, so the whole cycle would begin again.

In retrospect, the good sex I've had has always been with people I know.

Eventually I did manage to befriend a rather charming young man called Adrian, who was politicized and totally out. I think that's where a lot of my current ideas come from, he educated me from the beginning.

He was there at the very first gay society meeting I went to. He looked after me and it turned into a relationship. We ended up sharing a flat for a while, and I used to staple together the pages of the radical magazines he was compiling. I didn't understand all the issues at the time, but I think I learnt a lot as I went along.

I have always drawn strength from other people's confidence

in their sexuality. This partly explains my present involvement with the activist group OutRage!

I first went along to OutRage! to mock. I didn't believe in this stupid organization. However, I found a room full of sussed people who had rational reasons for what they were doing. They had thought through their ideas.

I'm sure that they had as many insecurities as I do, but they talked about sex and sexuality in such an upfront way, that I found it totally empowering. It is a strengthening charge for me. I draw energy from the meetings that carries me through my week.

TRENT, MIDLANDS

I'm not really an activist, but I would march if people were being persecuted. My world is quite comfy and I've never experienced homophobia.

I drove past Pride once, but it didn't look like my type of thing. It seemed a bit loud and threatening. I think I'm lucky because the world I move in is quite accepting. I like it when you don't have to come out to people, they just know.

TELLING THE WORLD

> Now I shout it from the highest hills,
> I even told the golden daffodils.
> At last my heart's an open door
> And my secret love's no secret any more.
>
> **DORIS DAY**

Once you have gone through the trauma of telling one person you are gay, it gets so much easier. Many lesbians and gay men feel that once they have fully accepted their sexuality they want the whole world to know. It's almost compulsive. Some of us rush around telling all our friends. Some send out a press release. After keeping a secret to yourself for so long, it can be such a relief to shout out loud . . .

SARAH, SUSSEX

Once I'd come out to one person, the gossip seemed to spread around the nurses' home like wildfire. One of my closest friends arrived at my door in tears, not because I was a lesbian but because I hadn't told her myself. Then she asked me if I fancied her, and when I reassured her I didn't, she sobbed, 'Why not?'

After this experience I decided that I wanted to do things on my own terms. So I went on a sort of coming out spree, telling all my friends and acquaintances in a bright and positive way. I don't know if I was shouting out, but I was certainly speaking very loudly and trying to celebrate my sexuality.

Some people would hang around the lesbians in the bar because they thought it was trendy and right-on. I was always friendly though, in case someone was trying to edge their way into the scene and get the strength to come out too. I do believe it's difficult and we shouldn't ever forget that.

MICHAEL, LONDON

As soon as I came out of the closet I became *really* gay, and I wanted everyone to know. I worked in a bar in Manchester, and on my first night I walked in and announced: 'Hello, I'm Michael, and I'm gay.'

I told everyone I met and I never had a bad reaction. I just got stronger and stronger as a gay person. Even if I went to the ice-cream man I managed to drop it in: 'One strawberry cornetto for a homosexual, please.'

When you're in the closet for years, you always think you

can't tell anyone because they'll just kick you and laugh and push you away.

It wasn't until seven years later that I went to something like Pride. When I left Manchester I went to the West Country and they don't tend to have many gay marches through Exeter.

AAMIR, WIMBLEDON

I really came out publicly in my second year at university. I went on this huge march in Manchester, against **Clause 28**, and doing that was brilliant for me. I felt as if I had arrived on the queer planet! I'd never been to Pride or anything before, so I was just amazed at what was going on.

I had a bit of a shit time at university to begin with. I was living in a hostel with eight other men, all rowdy straights, but friendly enough. Martin, my boyfriend, would come up every week, and we'd spend a furtive afternoon in the local seedy gay hotel. After a while I realized it was ridiculous to hide my relationship like this. So I told Martin to come to Manchester for the Clause 28 march, knowing that all my liberal straight friends were going.

Afterwards, they questioned me about Martin, clearly puzzled about seeing me with a strange man who was a different age and race to me. I simply said, 'He's my boyfriend,' and they couldn't believe it. Suddenly their attitude completely changed. I realized that their going on a gay march had been a completely naff, liberal, student thing to do, and that in reality, they had a problem with my sexuality. They couldn't accept that somebody they actually knew was queer. The fact that they had gone on the march and then reacted in this way made me feel sick.

Since then, I have decided that it is a mistake to hide your sexuality. Those straight friends of mine knew me for a whole year, and thought I was quite an open person. But all that time I was hiding my true self, and when I suddenly said, 'I'm gay,' they were shocked.

Nowadays, I make a point of announcing my sexuality almost as soon as I meet someone – 'Hello, I'm gay, can I have a pint of milk?' – that sort of thing. I'm out to everyone I work with, and I believe that if you're confident about your sexuality, people make less of an issue of it. Being gay is not just about what you do in bed, it is a huge part of your life. Coming out is the only way to be free as yourself, the person you really are.

IAN, WORTHING

In the sixth form, I was very brave and wrote an article for the college magazine. Amongst 400 students, I was the only out gay person, which I still find hard to believe. This article meant a lot to me, it felt like the most important thing I'd ever done. I even quoted Jimmy Somerville in it, which is pretty scary!

Prior to publication, I was summoned to the principal's office for a chat, during which he tried to say, 'We don't want this sort of thing.' But I was pretty assertive, saying that this was a student magazine and I was a student, so where's the problem? And so it got published, next to a picture of a naked man which my friend had drawn, and I was desperately proud of it.

PATRICK, BOURNEMOUTH

My most public coming out was done during my last year at college. Encouraged by my best friend Vanessa, I went along to the lesbian and gay society. It was dreadful. The dykes all sat in one corner bitching about the gay men, and the gay men all stood in the opposite corner bitching about each other. And this was supposed to be a cheese and wine party. Only one man came to speak to me, and he was the president.

Much as I hated it, I forced myself to go to the next meeting. It was there I decided that this group was going nowhere, and I had to change that. I got talking to one of the lesbians, who agreed with me. So between us we took that group, and transformed it into a popular, powerful and controversial force within the university. We even got the men and women talking to each other.

We organized events that got us mentioned in the gay press, and we invited Derek Jarman and Ian McKellen to speak at our college, before that became trendy. I considered these to be major achievements at my college, which was completely right-wing.

We were pretty high profile that year. At the freshers' fair, we craftily placed our stall between the drama society and the women's group, thereby ensuring we got twice as many members. We also got control of the stereo at this event, so everyone listened to two hours of gay music.

I was studying law, and I made sure that gay issues were discussed at every lecture. There isn't a section of British law that I didn't relate to lesbians and gay men. When I opened my mouth, people would groan as I introduced another hideous gay rights issue. And I never failed!

Part Three
Moving On

FAMILIES OF THE FUTURE

**I believe that children are the future,
treat them well and let them lead the way.**
WHITNEY HOUSTON

So what does the future hold? Lesbian and gay people are increasingly featured in the media, and are becoming a part of 'everyday' life. Heterosexuals have reported sightings of them as close as the local supermarket. Do we want to assimilate into the broader society, or safeguard our queer culture?

In the UK, the age of consent for gay men has been reduced by two years, but it remains unequal to the heterosexual law. Lesbians do not have an age of consent. But as everyone knows, they don't actually have sex, they just stroke each other's hair and read poetry in bed.

Homosexual couples cannot marry. Some would like to, and others feel that we should not be aping heterosexual institutions. Some of us have childhood dreams of floating up the aisle in a heavily laced dress – but it's usually only gay men who will admit to this fantasy.

Lesbians and gay men are getting involved in child-rearing, through either artificial/self-insemination or fostering. Do these queer families fit into society? Where will the homosexuals of future generations find themselves?

SUSAN, WINKLEIGH

I'd like to think that I might have children in the future. If I stay with my present girlfriend then we'll definitely have some. I feel that I don't want to be left out. If there are children to be had, I don't want to be the only one not having them. The only question is who to use as a donor. I have considered having a 'legitimate' baby with my gay husband, but he doesn't really like children.

SARAH, WORTHING

When I look to the future I think that queer families will become more common and be accepted by straight society. At present there is a growing generation of children raised by gay or lesbian parents. Many people, including some homosexuals, think that this is unnatural or wrong. But as the children grow up, those cynics will be forced to retract their words.

I know a lesbian couple who have a very happy and well-balanced five-year-old son, and two men who have a gay foster son. Homosexuals make the best parents, because every child is carefully planned and deliberated over for years. No lesbian gets pregnant by accident, then begrudgingly has the baby.

If I have a baby, my partner's parents might have trouble accepting it into their family. But kids are winners, and as soon as you present the little baby, people are drawn to it. Children bond families together.

JOE, ALABAMA

I guess that I have created my own queer family of the future. It's pretty radical, but not in the way that most people would expect.

I have always entertained the idea of marrying an English lesbian for the purpose of staying in the UK. I used to read the classified ads in the gay press with this in mind. One day I answered an advert placed by a lesbian. It caught my eye because she was asking for friendship as well as a 'mutually beneficial arrangement'. We met, and were immediately comfortable with each other.

129

Six months later we married, and I took her back home to meet my family. They don't know that I am gay. You have to remember that this is small town America. These people have never been out of the state. They are strictly religious and very conservative.

There isn't much of a gay scene in Alabama, but there is a bar where you can see one of the best Judy Garland impersonations in the world.

Me and my wife were very thorough about our arrangements. We got married in London, and then travelled to Alabama to meet the folks. This area is real bible-belt country, and as we got further into the state I could sense her unease. I think the sight of twenty-foot crosses on the hill made her nervous.

We decided to book into a hotel rather than have the stress of staying with the family. The big introductions took place at a restaurant, where we all had dinner, at 5.30pm.

Everyone knew that my wife was from England, but none of them had met an English person before (let alone a radical dyke). The children were worried that they would not be able to understand her. The adults had reassured them though, saying, 'She'll sound just like Mary Poppins, honey.'

They were intrigued when they met her asking questions like, 'Are there trees in London?' and, 'Do you all have seasons in England?'

My wife handled herself very well. We couldn't look at each other though, we would have just dissolved into laughter. It went according to plan, and they completely believed that we were husband and wife. I felt a bit guilty afterwards that I had fooled them so well.

The only problem was drink. Alcohol is a sin in this area. A man seen with a can of beer is considered to be halfway to hell. So of course the restaurant served no alcohol, and none of my family drink. As we left, my wife turned to me and said: 'Just get me a gin.'

I think the time is coming when I'm going to have to tell them the truth. The family are talking about saving up and coming to England to stay with me and my wife. She is not prepared to go this far, and I agree. I feel confident enough with myself now that if they freak out, I'll consider it their problem.

ISLA, LONDON

Queer families are definitely the families of the future. I have two young children and I don't know many straight parents. My partner helps with looking after the kids. She even babysits while I go out cruising, which is quite handy. I take my children to Lesbian Avengers meetings with me. They love it. My son is the only male member, but very proud!

JOSEPH, YORKSHIRE

I would really like to have children, and I know that I am capable of bringing up a child. I think that it's a possibility, either with another man, a lesbian or a straight woman. I feel confident about that.

I would like gays to integrate sensibly into society. Having children is such a good way to become part of the broader culture and to show people that we can do it as well as them. To rear a child is one of the most powerful things. To do that and be gay is to gain huge strength. Ignorant people need proof that we can be equally good parents.

You can live a fabulous gay life without children. But all men have an instinct to reproduce, not just straight men. I certainly get broody, and I think that is a natural part of life. The gay man who loves young children is still considered suspicious, which I hate, especially as it is known that most sexual abuse is perpetrated by straight men.

I don't feel that I identify with Pride much any more. This year, after the festival, the streets were littered with leaflets depicting testicles and penises. I don't think this is what Pride is about. It should be political.

KATHLEEN, ALASKA

I intend to have a child of my own when I am more settled. I'd like to get married to a woman and have a big ceremony. In Hawaii, same sex marriages are about to be made legal, so I could go there and do it. I would expect my family to be present, and I'd be angry if they weren't.

I used to be obsessed with coming out to absolutely everyone, but now I don't bother so much. The school I'm at is pretty homophobic and students there tend to gossip. I always have a kind of 'fuck you' attitude anyway, so if people have a problem with it, I don't really care.

FUTURE POSSIBILITIES

**Somewhere over the rainbow, way up high,
there's a land that I heard of, once in a lullaby.**

JUDY GARLAND

Some people feel that huge progress has been made in the last twenty-five years. Things are certainly easier for us than for our grandparents' generation, but does this mean they will get even better in the future?

Lesbians and gay men are coming out to their bosses, their doctors, their milkmen and their pets. Maybe, at some point, it won't be necessary to come out at all, as sexuality will cease to be an issue. The people in this section are certainly the optimists . . .

PATRICK, BOURNEMOUTH

Working in a City law firm isn't the easiest environment for a gay person. When I first started, I made a decision not to come out unless asked. The pressure was definitely on to conform. Eventually, I began hinting broadly at my sexuality. As the boss once again said to me, 'When you get married and become a partner . . . ,' I would reply, 'I don't think that will happen.' But that was as far as I went.

Now, I'm glad to say, things have changed. At work three of the fifteen solicitors are gay men, and we have complete monopoly. Whenever we all go out together, we insist on dragging them to some seedy gay club. All twelve of them stand politely at the bar while we three rip off our tops and freak out on poppers. This I call progress.

When I look to the future, I imagine that at some glorious point it will be less necessary to 'come out' as we do now. I think it will be something you mention along with where you live or the fact that you're left-handed. I think London will lead the way in this because, like all capitals, it attracts a more cosmopolitan, free-thinking crowd. Also it controls the country's media.

There will come a time, I hope, when lesbians and gay men can walk down the street holding hands. In some places you can already do this. It might raise an eyebrow, but usually on the face of a visiting tourist. And if anyone gives you hassle, they will be regarded as the freak, rather than the finger being pointed at you.

AAMIR, WIMBLEDON

When I look at society's attitude to gay people, I can see it changing, but very gradually. It is no longer acceptable to make homophobic comments, and in some areas things are altering radically. My partner and I have a gay foster son. To think that Social Services are acknowledging the benefits of placing gay kids with gay parents is amazing. All young people need to have good self-esteem, but gay kids in particular are constantly told they are abnormal, sick, perverted or disturbed. They need role models and someone just to tell them that there is nothing wrong with the feelings they are having, that being gay is part of you, a natural part of you, just like hair colour or the shape of your nose.

In terms of the future, the people in this country who are making the biggest changes are not the activists, the politicians or the workers in queer charities, but the average gay people – the queers who are out to their parents, their neighbours and out at work. The difference they make is earth-shattering. Most of the people who are prejudiced against us think that they don't know any lesbians and gays. The only way to combat homophobia is to come out to these people; to let them know that amongst their family, colleagues and friends there are queers lurking!

TODD, CHICAGO

I think it is inevitable that gay people will become a normal and full part of society. That is the goal we should have. We are one of the last minority groups to gain any power. We have an edge over other groups in that we are not all economically disadvantaged. Public morality is against us, rather than economics. But I am confident that things are going to change.

STEVEN, LANCASHIRE

On a personal level, my coming out has to be an ongoing process. This is because the lack of confidence that I have in my sexuality extends into other areas of my life. The two seem very interconnected, therefore I know that the more positive I can feel about being gay, the better everything will seem.

In one part of me I know that my career is going brilliantly, but I still feel insecure about it. I never allow myself to feel that I'm doing well. It's the same with being gay, I have this underlying sense of failure. Deep down I'm defensive about my sexuality. I think I almost overcompensate for it in some very upfront areas of my life, such as my work with OutRage! and having an obviously queer partner. In these situations, my sexuality has become an assertion, a statement, almost the reason for life itself.

Therefore, my coming out and shouting out will continue, until I can be as loud and as proud in the rest of my life as I am on an OutRage! demonstration.

CAROLYN, BIRMINGHAM

When I think of the future, I do feel quite optimistic. So many advances have been made over the last few years. I think television has contributed hugely to this. Soap operas and other primetime programmes can provide us with powerful role models.

I find it inspirational and therapeutic to watch gay characters speaking out. Their upfront behaviour can help people think through their unkind and ingrained prejudices. The fact that you can see these programmes before the watershed is quite amazing.

I also think it's brilliant that nowadays you can walk into Dillons or Waterstones and they have a section for lesbian and gay books. I really hope that society will become more tolerant as a result. It will then be harder for gay people to hide their true feelings. We will not be able to use the excuse, 'The whole world hates us,' as a reason for not coming out.

There's room for improvement in the gay world too. I sometimes feel that we don't make it very easy for people who are new to everything.

I think that the future should bring many different types of lesbians out into the open, which would be really positive. Even over the last twenty years here in Birmingham, I have seen much development. The bars do seem to be more diverse nowadays with various nights for different people: leather on Wednesdays, country and western on Thursdays, etc. There are definitely many more women around, but I still think that it is difficult to meet people.

I hope our language develops too. I hate the word 'lesbian'. It's a very cold word, I prefer to be called 'gay'. 'Dyke' is not any better, as it brings to mind harsh, leather-type women. And as for 'queer', I detest it. It makes me think of something unpleasant. I am clean and decent and not something only to be seen at night in strange places. Even the term 'lesbians and gay men' is quite dividing. We've got a role together, helping the rest of society who are struggling with us.

One of the things that I think society will find hard to accept is the idea of two women raising a child. I've never wanted children personally, but the argument I've heard around the staff dining table at school is that they wouldn't have a stable background, or that they would grow up hating men.

I don't think that is necessarily true because you can't make somebody gay by the way you bring them up. Take my childhood for example: four of us were brought up the same way, and yet one of us feels different. However, it's very easy to become a straight parent, at least a lesbian's child would be planned.

I like the idea of breaking down barriers, providing you can construct a new system that is good.

Some people say that it's easy when you're gay because you can meet someone, have a relationship, and then move on without the constraints of a marriage certificate. I think gay partnerships that survive must be even more special for that very reason; there are no manacles keeping the couple together, it's their choice. More choice would be a good thing to aim for in the future.

STEPHEN, IRELAND

I have a very idealistic view of the future. Michelangelo Signorile, in his book *Queer in America*, made a point which really stuck in my mind. He describes the current state of being queer as similar to being Jewish forty years ago; people hiding their sexuality is like Jews changing their names and anglicizing them. Then there came a historical point where the Jewish people reached a confidence and it became shameful to hide your Jewish credentials.

I have this hope that something similar could happen to the queer community. So, in my opinion, it is essential that those of us involved in activism continue trying to educate society.

We are currently at a stage where only a few people will stand up and be proud. My dream is that in the future it will be a matter of absolute shame to hide your sexuality.

BECKY, KENDAL

In the future there is going to be a whole generation of stroppy gay pensioners who have lived a totally out life. They will make a difference I hope. There aren't many out people in our grandparents' generation today.

I think the days of lesbian separatism are over really, there has been so much development between lesbians and gay men.

The media has really helped with gay visibility. The fact that lesbian characters are in soap operas on early evening television is great. Even if they are not particularly true to life, at least they are there.

137

THE FUTURE IS LESBIAN

**No one is going to give you power.
You have to take it.**

HARVEY MILK

Many lesbians feel that the gay scene has been male-dominated for too long. Dykes want to be their own force, and have a chance to express themselves. With the sudden media craze for 'lesbian chic', we have become hot property. Dykes grace the pages of the Sunday supplements and every respectable soap opera has its lesbian character, kiss, and controversy.

Lesbian strength is more than media hype, though: lesbians are out, strong and taking control. 1994 saw the formation of the London Lesbian Avengers which has provided inspiration, adrenalin and marvellous T-shirts to lesbians everywhere. Now all we have to do is take over the boys' bars . . .

JULIE, SOUTH WALES

I feel a bit disillusioned when I look to the future.

At the time of Clause 28 I was so fucking outraged that I got involved with activism. I stormed around the streets stamping my feet and shouting a lot. So did a great many other people.

But nowadays the London gay scene seems to be **Old Compton Street** and loads of dosh. The queer community has become so moneyed, and so unpolitical.

I think there are reasons for this. Basically, the sexual revolution has finally come for dykes. There's a hedonistic attitude amongst lesbians. They are celebratory and I don't blame them.

The fact is that, nowadays, gay women don't have to fight the old battles with 1970s feminists. They've got their sexual freedom and they're bloody well enjoying it. It's as if the dykes have taken over the party because gay men have been so badly hit by AIDS. I think that in another ten years a lot of women will get fed up with swishy bars and there'll be a political resurge.

But at the moment, America is so far ahead. There are women there who have spent the last decade working with AIDS, and now they're moving on to work with other health issues such as breast cancer.

The Lesbian Avengers in the US are just doing such fab things. I'd love to be working with women like that, but would there be the impetus here?

I know I'll get reinvolved with activism at some point. I'm far too mouthy to stay away forever.

RISHMA, EAST AFRICA

I think that things are becoming easier for us gay girls, especially since we are all over the television in soap operas. Some of the portrayals are inaccurate, but at least people are getting more used to the idea of lesbians. Eventually we will cease to be a novelty.

MAXINE, PRESTON

Even in the ten years that I've been out, I've seen dramatic changes. The fresh-faced, newly out baby-dykes appear to be getting younger and younger. They don't seem to feel the need to go through the bloke stage, which is inspiring. I hope this trend continues.

I think positive role models will become increasingly vital. I want to become a women's studies teacher, and I would consider my sexuality to be an integral part of my work. You can't separate the two.

The whole higher education system endeavours to make lesbian and gay lecturers an invisible part of the process. You can't distance yourself totally from what you teach. It's a highly subjective business and you need to put a lot of personal passion into your job.

Tutors can come out as left-wing, so why not as lesbians?

ASSIMILATION

Let me listen to me and not to them.

GERTRUDE STEIN

Opinion in the gay community is divided on this one. Should we cultivate and expand our own queer community, and be self-sufficient, or should we strive for acceptance within heterosexual society?

Many people believe that assimilation involves compromise on our part, and amounts to the same as going back into the closet, or at least having our behaviour dictated by a hostile society. The debate develops as, each year, numbers at Pride are increasingly swelled by 'sympathetic' straights. Do we welcome their support, or feel invaded? After all, they can kiss in the park any day of the year . . .

DON, ILLINOIS

One of the things I worry about is whether the gay community is going to be weakened by more people coming out. The community was built up and made strong because there was so much animosity towards lesbians and gay men. They were forced to come together as a group. With greater acceptance, I wonder if people will assimilate themselves into the broader culture, and we will lose that sense of community.

I haven't come out to any of my extended family. I've never felt that it was necessary to tell them, and my mum has kept my sexuality pretty much to herself. I have never talked to my brother about being gay. We have totally different lifestyles. He works in the straight pornography industry, erecting peep-show booths, and I'm a music librarian. So, no common ground there really. However, I now have a relationship that looks like it might be long-term, and I would like to take Steve home, which means coming out to relatives.

At college there is a great gay culture. There are four different groups, catering for all sections of the community, plus a coming out group which is obviously invaluable.

As for gay people having children, my good friend Frost and her partner Shannon have asked me for some sperm. It was a really big shock for me and I'm considering their proposal. I'm not sure if I would feel comfortable with a close friend having a child that is part mine. If it was someone I didn't know, I think I would feel better about the idea.

MICHAEL, GUILDFORD

In an ideal world, everyone would come out, then society would have to be more tolerant. Coming out is very powerful. Straight people need to see homosexuals in their workplace, at the shops and in ordinary set-ups.

I do find the concept of the 'gay community' a bit disturbing, though. The only thing that links us is the silent understanding of our sexuality: a nod and a wink. What people tend to forget is that within this community there are men and women from a huge range of backgrounds and lives. The gay community is the same as the straight community – it doesn't exist. It is dangerous to think that we must all like each other because we share a sexuality.

The age of consent will go down to sixteen at some point, I am sure. The trouble is that most of our MPs were raised in the age of ignorance, when homosexuality was illegal, underground and disgusting. Since 1967, gays have become more visible. Straight people have gay friends and things are changing. Personally, I am finding it easier to be gay. I don't know if that is due to my acquired wisdom, or to the fact that I don't associate with bigots.

I don't like the thought of ghettos, I think our world should merge with the broader community. Having said that, I do like Old Compton Street. I just wish that we didn't need to have it.

Gay Pride is an important political statement because we still suffer inequality. It's the only day when I can put my arms round my boyfriend and not feel threatened. We are the majority for a day. As long as we have an unequal age of consent, as long as we can't walk the streets holding hands, and as long as we have to go to gay clubs to be ourselves, then Pride must continue. When these barriers are down, we won't need our annual celebration. Every day will be a gay day.

HOPE FOR THE FUTURE?

**The way I see it,
if you want the rainbow,
you gotta put up with the rain.**
DOLLY PARTON

The next section concerns those who have a slightly more pessimistic view of the future – or perhaps they are the realists, who have wisely chosen not to expect too much.

It is certainly true that 'society' can be perturbed by things that rock the boat, and homosexuality seems to be very threatening to many people. We have governments and laws to overcome, then there is the church, with its strict morals backed up by God Herself. Will we ever be welcomed out of the closet with open arms . . . ?

FI, LEICESTER

I know it seems cynical, but I really don't think that anything will change for gay people within the next decade. Every day, lesbians and gays have to make decisions about whether it is safe to come out. This hasn't altered in the last ten years, so I'm pretty negative about the future. In some ways, being gay has become more fashionable, but that's all very shallow and it doesn't bring about a huge cultural shift. Everyone is assumed to be heterosexual unless proven otherwise, and that will never change.

STEVE, GEORGIA

I think that there will always be segments of the community who will stay in the closet. There are areas such as the arts where being gay is acceptable, almost expected. Some professions on the other hand, will not tolerate it. In my lifetime, sexuality will continue to be an issue.

I'm involved with many AIDS projects in New York. There is a tremendous camaraderie in these areas. I'd like to think that if the AIDS crisis is ever over, all this energy and organization will be channelled into something else. My friends have told me that this won't happen; that, post-AIDS crisis, everyone will go straight back to the dance floors and the promiscuous sex, and carry on where they left off. I hope my friends are wrong.

I would like more people to get involved in going on marches and supporting the gay community. I love it. It gives me the chance to wear pearls and go out in the sunshine.

VICKY, WEST WALES

I think it will always be difficult to come out in Wales. There are areas where people will never see *The Pink Paper*, where others live in fear.

Wales is very traditional and heterosexual. The women are mainly seen as matriarchal figures, and it's very difficult to break the mould. I can't see it changing in the future because of the chapel culture.

I would never have my own baby, I couldn't bear the pain. I might be involved in raising someone else's child, but there is no legal protection for people in these scenarios. If the relationship breaks up, I think it can be very traumatic for all involved.

SAMANTHA, LEEDS

Looking to the future, I don't think my mum will ever tell anyone that I'm a lesbian.

Once, when my aunt was preparing for her daughter's wedding, she turned to my mum, and in a comforting tone whispered, 'Don't worry, Samantha will be next.'

'I don't think Samantha will ever get married,' replied my mum.

I thought this was quite bold, but my aunt wasn't impressed. She snapped back at my mum, 'Well, I don't think you'll help her find a husband with that attitude. We've got to be positive about these things.'

Mum and I exchanged silent glances.

NIGEL, ROTHERHAM

I live in Barcelona now. I love it here, but I've come to realize that it isn't quite the gay paradise that everyone imagines.

In Valencia, lesbians and gays can now adopt babies, but this is a very new thing and there is still a hell of a long way to go. Gay people don't seem to fight as much here, they just get on with it. They don't expect their families to know, they just lead two separate lives, which never coincide. It's deceitful. I blame the Catholic Church.

ASSUME NOTHING

I can tell,
you think you know me well,
but you don't know me.

RAY CHARLES

Dare to dream, and imagine for a moment a world in which you didn't need to come out. Every time you met someone new, or started a job, you wouldn't have to worry about the 'right time' to announce your sexuality, or struggle to avert personal questions.

In our supposedly liberal society, it is customary to assume that everyone is straight until proven otherwise. While this state of affairs remains, lesbians and gay men are being forced to undergo a continual decision-making process – is it safe to come out?

IAN, WORTHING

I hope that there will come a time when one's sexuality is not assumed. People are definitely thought of as straight unless they contradict the ugly rumours. Changing attitudes in this country is going to take some time. Killing vast numbers of Tories would probably help, as would shutting down the *Daily Mail*, *The Times* and *Telegraph*. Britain is so hung up about sex that coming out at any age is very difficult. If only people would realize that homosexuality is not just about what you do in bed, or in **Russell Square** for that matter.

SUZANNE, AUSTRALIA

Nowadays, I don't think that young people are pressured into coming out. They haven't grown up with the same rules as my generation, so they don't feel obliged to define their sexuality.

ANTHONY, ABERGAVENNY

Nowadays, I don't necessarily come out to people in big, heavy confessional sessions. I don't really feel the need for this any more. I just act as myself, and people guess or find out indirectly through general conversation. For example, if a colleague asks me what I did last night, I might say, 'I went to see that new film with my boyfriend, have you seen it yet?' I don't make a big deal out of it. I just state the truth and leave any further discussion to them.

I do know, however, that I'm very privileged to be working where I am. It's a protected environment and things might be extremely different if I worked elsewhere.

Looking to the future, I wish more people could be lucky enough to have such a positive working environment. I think it's very important.

TO HAVE AND TO HOLD

**We're going to the chapel,
and we're gonna get married . . .**
THE DIXIECUPS

Marriage, everyone will agree, is a heterosexual institution.
Two people make a public declaration of their love, have a
party, then rush off on honeymoon to start making babies.
But there is more to marriage than dressing like a meringue
and sitting through long speeches. Many gay couples would
like to cement their relationship with a ceremony, a large
ring and copious amounts of alcohol. Gay couples have no
partnership rights. We cannot be each other's legal next of
kin.

Surely, if queer marriages were legalized it would be a
huge advance? Or maybe this is just another example of lesbians and gay men trying to imitate straight society . . .

ROSIE, STAFFORDSHIRE

Me and my girlfriend would like to get married one day. Many
gay people think that this is conforming to a heterosexual stereotype, but I disagree. A marriage ceremony is whatever you make
it. Two people committing to each other in public is a great thing.
We want to declare our love to the world and have a big party
into the bargain. I hate it when gay people say that homosexuals
shouldn't get married. I'm not forcing anyone to get married, gay
or straight, but everyone should have the option.

MICHAEL, LONDON

I think we have a long way to go before a thirteen-year-old
can say, 'Yeah, I'm a lesbian,' and be completely accepted. That

147

would be true equality. There are so many gay people around, and lots of them are having kids, so it has to be mentioned in schools. Gay issues should be raised with all children.

A friend of mine recently came out at work, after years of being in the closet. He later found out that his boss is homophobic, and he's been refused every promotion since. This sort of thing has to stop.

The older generation still think that we are deviants, so we have to fit into society at some point and show them that we are just like everyone else.

I think that gay couples should have some sort of legal partnership deal, but not a marriage with vows and everything. That would just be copying the heterosexuals. We could still have a ring, because we all like a bit of gold about our person. I think gay couples having a ceremony should wear matching outfits in the freedom colours, and have a massive all-day party to celebrate. I don't think that having an anniversary of the day you met is the same as the anniversary of the day you committed permanently to each other.

MICHAEL, GUILDFORD

I am opposed to marriages in church, I think it's hypocritical. However, I would like gay couples to be able to have a blessing, and a legal status. Gay relationships are not seen as being the same as heterosexual ones, and that is a grave injustice.

POSTSCRIPT

If you have enjoyed this book and feel that you would like your own coming out story considered for future editions, please send it to the author, c/o The Editor, Sexual Politics List, Cassell plc, Wellington House, 125 Strand, London WC2R OBB.

All information received will be treated confidentially, guaranteeing the anonymity of the contributor, if desired.

GLOSSARY OF TERMS

AC/DC: dated British slang term for bisexual.

ACT UP (AIDS Coalition To Unleash Power): direct action group founded in New York in 1987 to campaign around AIDS and HIV issues. It formed because, after six years of the epidemic, little medical progress had been made. ACT UP London was formed in 1989.

Albert Kennedy Trust: provides housing, support and advice for young lesbian and gay teenagers, who are homeless or living in a hostile environment.
23 New Mount St, Manchester M4 4DE. Tel: 0161 953 4059
Box 13, Lower Richmond Rd, London SW15 1HJ.
Tel: 0181 780 5505.

Boy's Own Story: 1982 novel by gay writer Edmund White. It is considered the ultimate coming out novel for gay men.

Boystown: the heart of Chicago's gay community. Home of the Guppies (gay upwardly mobile professional people).

CHE: Campaign for Homosexual Equality. British group for lesbian and gay rights. In the early 1970s it had a rather fractious relationship with GLF, which it saw as being too extreme. In 1974, CHE made a commitment to more militant forms of activity, and consequently the two groups combined their different elements much more effectively.

Clause 28: part of the 1988 Local Government Bill which prohibited local authorities from using public funds to 'promote' homosexuality. A huge campaign was mounted by lesbian and gay groups, and there were demonstrations across the country. Most memorable amongst these was a group of lesbians abseiling from the visitors' gallery into the House of Lords, and dykes disrupting a live broadcast of the BBC six o'clock news. The tabloid headline 'Beeb man sits on lesbian' will go down in queer history. Despite these actions, the bill was passed and the clause became Section 28 of the Local Government Act.

CND: Campaign for Nuclear Disarmament.

Cottage: gay slang for a public toilet where men meet for sex.

Criminal Justice Act: Brought the homosexual age of consent for men down to eighteen, despite a large public campaign for an equal age of consent at sixteen. It also acknowledged the crime of male rape by including anal intercourse.

Daisy chain: slang term from the 1950s for occasions when more than two men engage in anal sex simultaneously.

Gay Liberation Front: radical lesbian and gay organization that was set up in New York following the Stonewall riots of 1969. The first British meeting was held in the London School of Economics in 1970. Their magazine was entitled *Come Together*.

Gay News: British gay newspaper founded in 1972. In 1974, it was taken to court over a cover photo of two men kissing, and again in 1977, when it was prosecuted for blasphemy. Published fortnightly, the last issue was in April 1983.

Greenham Common: in the 1980s, women's peace camp outside nuclear base. Women from all over the country lived there in tents and demonstrated against nuclear weapons. Their presence kept the issue in the public arena. Lesbians were rife!

Heaven: the largest gay nightclub in Europe, situated in London's West End.

Homophobia: fear or hatred of homosexuals. Great homophobes of our time include Margaret Thatcher and anyone working for the *Daily Mail*.

Labrys: double-headed axe used as a symbol for lesbianism. Origins associated with Amazon armies.

Lesbian and Gay Switchboard: London branch set up in 1974.

Helpline, providing a wide range of services, information and support; lesbian plumbers, gay house-shares, a listening ear or a vital fashion tip. Local switchboard numbers can be obtained from London lesbian and gay switchboard, or from your local phone book.
London Switchboard: 0171 837 7324. Twenty-four-hour service.

Lesbian Avengers: lesbian direct action group founded in New York in the 1990s. A London chapter was started in 1994, which has captured the imagination of straight journalists everywhere.

Lesbian Strength: annual lesbian march in London prior to Pride. The final march took place in 1988.

Old Compton Street: in London's Soho, it has a high concentration of male-oriented gay businesses. It is the UK equivalent of Christopher Street in New York or the Castro district in San Francisco.

Operation Spanner: name given to the undercover monitoring of a group of gay men by the Obscene Publications Squad. The men made home videos of themselves having sadomasochistic sex. The police eventually swooped and the men were taken to court in December 1990. There it was decided that under British law, consent is no defence for violence. (Boxing matches had obviously slipped their minds.) The men were given prison sentences for their activities and the case continues in the European Court.

Oranges Are Not The Only Fruit: 1985 novel by British lesbian writer Jeanette Winterson. Based on her own experiences as a young lesbian being raised by a fanatically religious mother within the evangelical church.

OutRage!: British direct action group set up in 1990. The group associates itself with queer politics and theatrical demonstrations.

Peter Tatchell: Stood as Labour Party candidate in the now infamous Bermondsey by-election of 1983. Prominent member of OutRage! and formerly of ACT UP London. 'Peggy' is also a vegetarian.

151

Pink Paper: free weekly British newspaper for lesbians and gay men. Distributed nationwide.

Pride: annual lesbian and gay march and festival, first held in Britain in August 1971 when a small crowd organized by the GLF marched from Marble Arch to Trafalgar Square. The attendance level in 1995 was in the region of 200,000.

Russell Square: a central London cruising ground, more urban than Hampstead Heath and less notorious. Every city in the world has its equivalent outdoor space where men meet for sex.

Sappho: magazine produced in the 1970s by London-based lesbian group of the same name. Sappho was involved in demonstrations with GLF and organized donor inseminations for lesbians. The group still meets, though the magazine is no longer published.

Sexual Offences Act 1967: following recommendations made in the Wolfenden report, it legalized consensual sex between men over the age of twenty-one, in private. This law applied only in England and Wales and did not include the British Armed Services or the merchant navy. Lesbian sex was not mentioned.

SM: sadomasochism. The giving or receiving of pain during sexual activity.

Steven Carrington: golden gay boy from American soap *Dynasty*. His combination of angst and beauty inspired gay men everywhere.

Transvestism: wearing clothes considered appropriate to the opposite sex. This behaviour is not necessarily linked to homosexuals. (They just do it with a lot more style.)

Zap: undercover operation in which a selected homophobe is taken by surprise and publicly exposed. These zaps are meticulously planned and invariably effective. And everyone gets their picture in the papers.

ACT OUT: DRAMA SECTION

This section is aimed at anyone who regularly works with young people: youth leaders, teachers, youth-club workers, etc.

It contains ideas and suggestions that could help to facilitate some work around the area of sexuality. This could range from a discussion looking at homophobia in society to a more interactive drama workshop around the sensitive issue of coming out.

Obviously, different groups will have varying needs – a lesbian and gay youth group is going to be working on a different level to a more mixed youth club. However, I do think that adults who work with young people have a responsibility to be aware of homophobia in these environments. Left unchallenged, it can eat away at young people's self-worth, and we end up with a community of very damaged individuals.

Through my theatre work over the last ten years, I have come to realize the versatility of drama games and exercises. They can be invaluable tools, allowing you to explore real-life situations within the confines of a safe environment.

I have run sessions and workshops around the themes of coming out, sexuality, and choice, and have always received very positive feedback, particularly on the use of roleplay.

Workshop Outline

It is difficult to give general guidelines for all groups. However, it is inappropriate to launch straight in to roleplays. A well structured workshop will build up to this type of activity.

153

Clearly it is very important that the participants enjoy themselves, otherwise they will have no desire to commit to similar sessions in the future. I would therefore recommend beginning with some introductory 'getting to know you' type exercises. These break down barriers and introduce a relaxed and fun atmosphere. If you are not experienced in this type of work, many helpful texts exist. I particularly recommend *Impro* by Keith Johnstone.

A productive way of introducing the roleplay idea is to gently ease into a game of 'Freeze Improvisation', which has been popularized by programmes such as *Whose Line Is It Anyway?*

Freeze Improvisation

Two willing volunteers (A and B) are given a situation and an opening line. They start to act out a scene, and then, at any point, the workshop facilitator shouts 'Freeze!' A third participant (C) then enters the scene and takes the *exact physical position* of one of the actors already involved, let's say B. Actor B then leaves the stage area, leaving the new couple, A and C, to perform.

However, *as each new person becomes involved a new scene begins*. Therefore, C must bring a fresh idea into the scene, one that makes sense within the context of the physical position s/he was obliged to assume.

For example, if A and B were looking for the proverbial contact lens, and were both on their hands and knees when the facilitator called 'Freeze!', then C (having assumed the position) might decide that they are now in a yoga class, members of a new cult, toddlers playing – anything *except* looking for a contact lens.

The best way to see how it works is to try it. A lot of

drama is about giving people permission to play, letting them use their imagination and creativity.

Pick a role, any role . . .

The wonderful thing about roleplay is that it's accessible and non-threatening: you don't have to be a performer, and to a certain extent theatrical choice is lessened. A character is 'given' and you put on the persona like a hat. The setting is also predetermined, so your main concern is how the character behaves and what they say.

This method can allow you to explore the full range of possibilities the situation offers. The facilitator can rewind the action, fast-forward or press the pause button. It's not real life, so the luxury of second attempts is allowed. The participants can explore different approaches: 'What would happen if . . . ?' 'Let's change the ending and see how it feels . . . ?

Roleplay can be a very constructive way of exploring potentially difficult situations such as coming out. Young people can develop different arguments, and practise being assertive. Obviously, there is no guarantee that your words will be reproduced exactly when you are in the real-life situation, but you will be more likely to remember some of the things you wanted to say if you have been through it before.

The workshop leader should provide some scenes to get the roleplays under way, then, if they feel confident, the group will have situations to suggest. Feel free to use any of the scenarios outlined in this book. Some of the interviews actually contain dialogue, written in script form, and these may be useful starting points.

Examples of this type of dialogue can be found in the following stories:

Anthony, Abergavenny – p.4

If you use these lines to start scenes, you can continue them in your own words. A final thought: some of the stories in this book are sad, some are traumatic, but some are also funny, either at the time or in retrospect. Humour makes difficult subjects accessible, and can be part of a coping mechanism. Don't be afraid of using this in your roleplays. Good Luck.

If you are interested in booking the two woman show *There Must Be Fifty Ways To Tell Your Mother*, or would like to find out more about our workshop programme, then please contact:

Off-Limits Theatre Company,
59 Queens Gate,
South Kensington,
London, SW7 5JP.
Tel: 0171 225 3692.